Praise for *The Peace Seeker* . . .

"Susan Gilmore's intimate understanding of the evangelical church
with the people within and around her church experience, gives credenc
in-depth knowledge of the bigotry that exists within this tradition. H
and struggle are palpable as she seeks to discern where God is wit
circumstances of her life. Anyone who has an interest in spirituality,
sexuality, the church, biblical scholarship, or sociology will find much ...
book to stimulate their thinking, inspire their heart, and challenge their views."

—**Christine Y. Wiley**
Pastor, Covenant Baptist United Church of Christ, Washington, DC

"Many Christian churches inflict untold damage on their members who
are LBGTIQ loving people. This woman's story is a testament to the power
of goodwill to confront even the most pernicious discrimination."

—**Mary E. Hunt, cofounder and codirector of**
Women's Alliance for Theology, Ethics and Ritual (WATER)

"Susan Gilmore has written a morally audacious, searingly honest, and
profoundly consoling account of her journey to bridge the distance between
whom she loves and the path of evangelical Christianity. Read it to learn how
far the human heart can reach to find God buried under fear and prejudice.
Read it, weep, and cheer at the glory of the human spirit."

—**Rabbi Malka Drucker, founding rabbi of HaMakom and**
author of *White Fire: A Portrait of Women Spiritual Leaders in America*

"Susan Gilmore's story is a blessing to gay and lesbian Christians and their
straight allies. It engages the reader in a conversation about love as the
essence of the Christian narrative: how we love, whom we love, and the
effects love has on rigid institutions. Her story offers hope to others on
the journey."

—**Rev. Dr. Sharon R. Graff**
Lead pastor, Gloria Dei Church, Huntingdon Valley, PA

"Ms. Gilmore's cause is a human rights moment for the church. It asks heart- and soul-searching questions in a spirit built solidly on the principles of her faith. The answer: love, acceptance, forgiveness, and community. This book will shock and propel controversy, spiritual dissonance, and hopefully thoughtful dialogue in the religious community."

—**Kathleen Zeiss, BS, MEd**
Educational consultant

"Susan Gilmore has taken a risk by sharing her story of being a homosexual in a heterosexual dominated world. Her story is important and should be read."

—**Marvin G. Baker**
Director, Gay Christian Fellowship

"Susan Gilmore's book tells the familiar human story of love and heartache as it has unfolded in her world as a gay evangelical Christian. The church needs her voice at this moment. Poignant, honest, brave, and compelling, *The Peace Seeker* confronts us with the prophetic question of how ready we are to heed Jesus's call and love our homosexual neighbor as we love ourselves."

—**J. R. Daniel Kirk**
Associate professor, Fuller Theological Seminary

"Susan E. Gilmore has given the church what it so desperately needs in the midst of our fractured theological debates over LGBT issues: a passionate, honest, behind-the-scenes story that helps us recapture the humanity of everyone involved in these battles over theology and morality."

—**Ed Cyzewski**
Author of *A Christian Survival Guide: A Lifeline to Faith and Growth*

THE PEACE SEEKER

One Woman's Battle in the
Church's War on Homosexuality

SUSAN E. GILMORE

PEACE SEEKER PRESS
FAIRVIEW VILLAGE, PENNSYLVANIA

Published by:

PEACESEEKER PRESS
PO Box 38
Fairview Village, PA 19409-0038
www.thepeaceseeker.com

Editor: Ellen Kleiner

Book design and production: Angela Werneke

Cover and interior art: Paul Hillman

Printed in the United States of America

PUBLISHER'S CATALOGING-IN-PUBLICATION DATA

Gilmore, Susan E.

The peace seeker : one woman's battle in the church's war on homosexuality / Susan E. Gilmore. — Fairview Village, Pennsylvania : Peaceseeker Press, 2015.

pages ; cm.

ISBN: 978-0-615-96692-2 (paperback)

ISBN: 978-0-692-22224-9 (eBook)

Summary: A memoir to bring awareness of those suffering that call themselves Christian and gay; to bring hope to the victims and peace between warring factions.—Publisher.

1. Gay activists—Religious life. 2. Toleration—Religious aspects—Christianity. 3. Social acceptance—Religious aspects—Christianity. 4. Homophobia—Religious aspects—Christianity. 5. Homosexuality—Religious aspects—Fundamentalist churches. 6. Homosexuality—Religious aspects—Evangelical Church. 7. Gilmore, Susan E. I. Title.

BV4596.G38 G55 2015   2014902792

261.8/35766--dc23   1501

1 3 5 7 9 10 8 6 4 2

To the silent who sit among us

ACKNOWLEDGMENTS

With appreciation that words cannot express, to Patti, who has sacrificed countless hours of together time. She has been a constant source of encouragement in helping me bring to fruition a book that has become our shared passion. With thanks to my sister, who has lived a lifetime of loving me well. With gratitude to the leaders of my church, who, despite what they had been taught, were brave enough to look once more. And lastly, to God, who has put it in my heart to write what I have experienced so that others may find peace.

CONTENTS

INTRODUCTION

This is the story of my double life—one in which I struggled alone for many years not realizing there were thousands of others anonymously by my side. We stand side by side in rows of hundreds and groups of thousands, people who until now have remained mostly silent. It is time for the silence to be broken, for our stories to be told. But there is a serious problem: to be the one who breaks the silence, to be the one who tells our tale scares me to death.

I tell my story after forty years of being in two opposing worlds that clash with rage and judgment, one world representing the belief system defining who I am in the universe and the other reflecting the identity I have confirmed as my true self. Standing with one foot in each of two worlds has led to a lifetime of secrecy and fear, but I can no longer remain silent. I am a Christian homosexual. And the God of love has put it in my heart to attempt to bring these two enemy worlds together to seek peace. After many years of seeking, I have reconciled my two worlds and found my long-sought-after peace. Now I yearn to help others seek the peace I struggled so hard to find.

For what seems like an eternity, the Christian church has possessed a heavily guarded, sealed box. It is made not of wood or steel but of something far more impenetrable: doctrines of the church regarding its beliefs on homosexuality. According to many scholars, the Christian church's regard for the homosexual lifestyle shifted from tolerance to intolerance and then eventually to hatred in the fifteenth century. The box contains the errant thoughts and prejudices of five centuries, permitting church leaders and members to ostracize, demean, and criminalize their own.

This box must be opened, the contents examined, and its errant beliefs changed so more pain is not inflicted on homosexual believers in the future.

Telling my story is an attempt to open the box in order to seek peace between the church and Christian homosexuals. The box is full of ugly insinuations and declarations, but it must be opened or change will never occur. Once it is opened, it will be seen that the contents are formidable from the bigotry of the ages. But the Christian church must plumb the depths of the box and its contents be brought into the light, exposing the darkness of prejudice. It is time for the Christian church to reexamine the scriptures and look into the eyes of homosexuals who have been alienated, forced to live a secret life in two worlds despite their love of Jesus and their wish to serve God.

While seeking to reconcile the two worlds I lived in, I immersed myself in personal research—on the Internet and through Bible study. When using the Internet, I was struck by the immensity of the issues connected with homosexuality and Christianity. The word *homosexuality* led to 189,000 entries, making me wonder why this is such a hot topic and so divisive. The entries seemed to fall into five main categories: the erotic, the Christian response, the response to the Christian response, theories and strategies for changing homosexuals to heterosexuals, and psychological findings about homosexuality. We all know or can imagine the erotic entries, such as advertisements for "hard male muscles seeking larger harder male muscles." In connection with the Christian response categories, some sites seemed to indicate that Christians are using homosexuality as a scapegoat for the immoral path the entire Western world is taking.

Christians are called to be "salt and light" in the world, to season the earth with goodness and do what is right amidst much degradation and an increase in ungodlike behaviors. But instead of continuing to do what is right and showing goodness, many conservative, right-wing Christians have become unnerved by the lack of restraint that is all around them and have turned to politics, self-righteously voicing their opinions about how the world should be and attempting to force others into their moral molds. They are trying desperately to hold back the tide of modern societal changes. They long for the America of yesterday, the Ozzie and Harriet 1950s world when families stayed together and attended church on Sunday mornings, when there was prayer in schools, and no one flinched when God was mentioned socially or at work. But they cannot hold back the tide and, frustrated, have made homosexuals the perfect focus of rage for their thwarted efforts.

Despite their politics and harsh rhetoric, the peace seeker in me can actually feel the pain and frustration of these evangelical Christians. They want others to come to know the God they love, but all they see is the world turning further and further away from him and becoming contrary to everything God intended.

But so many Evangelicals are self-righteous in their efforts to win others over to their beliefs that most people in their presence can't see the real Jesus anymore—that meek, eternal, soft-spoken, almighty, loving, sacrificial God-man. Jesus called us "to love our neighbor as ourselves," "to judge not that we would not be judged," "to be in the world, not of it." Instead, many evangelical Christians today seem the opposite of what they were called to be. In scripture, Christians are never called to point out other people's faults or sins. They are called to love, to show by example that God is the way to an abundant life, to point people toward Jesus and God and let him change what he thinks is necessary, to do good and to be charitable. Politics were not a part of Jesus's agenda. Regarding taxes, he said, "render unto Caesar that which is Caesar's," never claiming any money for himself. When the people wanted him to be king, he said, "my kingdom is not of this world." While Christians should continually stand up for what is right, they must always remember that this world is not ever going to be heaven. As long as humankind has free will, God will allow people to choose. Christians wish humankind would pick God and godly pursuits, but these days it seems that fewer and fewer choose to invite him into their lives.

As a result of all these developments, Christians need to find their roots again. Their lights need to shine—lights of kindness, patience, and joy that this planet needs to point others toward God.

I myself am an evangelical Christian. Not only was I was deeply entrenced in the Evangelical system of belief, but my story bears the mark of being born again and the forgiveness that Christ offers. Other Evangelicals will have to judge for themselves whether my conclusions about Christianity and homosexuality are accurate. This book is for them.

Others may know someone who, because of media focus on homosexuality, has come out of the closet to proclaim their identity. Maybe that person is a member of their family or church community, and they are shocked and saddened that the individual has succumbed to the way of the world. They do not know whether to run or reach out. They are torn between believing that the individual cannot possibly be a true believer and knowing that the person is. This book is for them.

Others have seen debates between the religious and the gays as a weekly subject on television, and have been appalled by the injustice they have witnessed. They cannot see why the debates persist because they have always believed that people's sexual orientation is determined at birth. This book is for them.

Many homosexuals have said, "Enough," and decided never to go to church again because they do not feel wanted or accepted there. Rather than feel judged or shamed by the misinformed, they have given up worship services where they once gathered strength from God and the church community. This book is for them.

Still others sit in church each week wrestling with their own sexual identity. They sing worship songs from their souls, on fire with love for God, yet wonder what might happen if those seated nearby learned the truth about who they are. They may get through Sundays unscathed by the pastor's teaching, but the day the sermon turns to homosexuality as sin or sexual depravity, they hope their facial expressions do not reveal their discomfort and doubts. This book is for them.

Personally, I was haunted by such doubts. My thoughts and emotions about my sexual identity would swing wildly. Despite the teachings of my church, I would spend some days certain it was okay to live a homosexual lifestyle, that God had not made a mistake. But come morning I would awaken wondering if I was completely wrong and that my soul had been deceived.

When someone becomes a believer in Christ, the Bible explains, the Holy Spirit comes and lives within them. The Holy Spirit's basic role in our lives is to guide, comfort, and convict. The first two functions bring joy, but conviction, best described as the pointing out of sins and aiding in their removal, is also necessary so that the person might eliminate those burdens from their life.

Many Christians who believe homosexuality is wrong may have already arrived at a conclusion about my spiritual status. Some might think that I cannot possibly be a true believer or that I have managed to somehow "squelch" the Holy Spirit. I would like to set the record straight on both accounts. I am an authentic, saved, born-again Christian. And I have been convicted of sin in my life by the Holy Spirit dwelling within me and felt the pain associated with that experience. But when it came to my homosexuality I could never really be certain whether what I had been taught was true. No matter how much my church and its leaders told me of the Bible's stand on homosexuality, uncertainty plagued me. No matter how many times I read the passages that seemed pertinent and prayed for deliverance, I knew there had to be something missing. I wanted to believe the pastors' interpretations of the scriptures on homosexuality, and I wished to have the Bible's living power change me. However, instead doubt racked my soul for close to thirty years. As a Baptist, I knew there had to be a missing piece to bridge the gap between what I felt about my authentic self and what the church taught about the sin of homosexuality, so I set off in search of it. That search would take me on a journey, one that started when I was very young, before I fully realized that I had embarked on it, and lasted until I found the missing piece, which allowed me to finally attain peace.

Most people who know my story cannot believe I would still go to church after many years of feeling ostracized and demeaned by church elders and members. My tale usually rates on the reaction scale between disgust and outrage. To know the pain of those years is to know my heart, a heart that loves God and wants to please God above all else in this world. In my story there is laughter and heartache, setbacks and personal growth. My story is not over, but for now the peace I have longed for and fought for has been won.

I tell my tale as an example for those who have had a similar experience and also for the silent army to persevere on the path to truth, as well as for those who aren't of my sexual persuasion, with the hope they may gain understanding, which is the key to mercy. To all, I am a peace seeker who wishes others peace.

THE PEACE SEEKER

CHAPTER 1

First Clues: Barbie and Cher

SOME OF MY FIRST CLUES ABOUT MY SEXUAL IDENTITY came from the daily sources of childhood entertainment. Barbie, goddess of the doll world, made her appearance in the early sixties dressed to the nines, and I was among her congregation of worshipers. Barbie was not just another doll; she was the gift of choice for little girls everywhere who adored the synthetic high priestess of fashion. I was proud of my collection of nine shapely blondes, brunettes, and redheads, a bevy of beauties that no little girl in the neighborhood could rival. I had no control over the growing population; Barbie seemed to multiply with every birthday and Christmas. And no self-respecting six-year-old girl could be without a carrying case, or three, full of accessories and drawers stuffed with the latest fashions. I spent hours posing Barbie in front of her aluminum foil mirror, admiring her well-put-together ensembles.

Yet even though my closet looked like a shrine to Mattel, I wasn't big on playing with dolls. I liked the clothes and the creativity of putting the outfits together, but after that I wasn't quite sure what to do with the Barbies. Their weird tippy-toe feet were perplexing, looking to me like a form of torture. I spent hours pondering those feet shaped like flesh-colored deformed birds, wondering if Barbie had stock in a large high heel manufacturer.

Ken, Barbie's boyfriend, was a nonentity to me. While my girlfriends would dress him and walk him down the aisle with Barbie, enacting their imaginary wedding day, I ignored him, keeping him in the carrying case rather than making him part of my play. I didn't dislike Ken or entertain thoughts of banning him from the harem; I just could never seem to fit him into the context of the glamorous life Barbie led. His black pants, white shirt, and occasional sweater were not enough to hold my interest. Ken seemed like that quiet, plastic type, boring and not worth the time, while Barbie, built like a top-heavy and curvaceous supermodel, held my attention. Even at six I enjoyed the beauty of the female body. This was not sexual; it was purely aesthetic. Her slender arms and tiny waist made my young mind conclude that women must be the pinnacle of God's creation.

In the 1970s when I was thirteen, the TV event called *The Sonny & Cher Comedy Hour* also drew my attention and gave me the first glimpse into who I might be. This musical variety hour was America's introduction to the pop-rock culture. Sonny and Cher were introduced as a couple but were so oddly paired that most viewers could not understand their mutual attraction. Sonny was a long-haired hippy type complete with John Lennon wannabe glasses and shaggy sheepskin vests, while Cher was a raven-haired beauty who wore gorgeous gowns and owned the stage. Hand in hand they walked toward the camera, illuminated by sweeping spotlights. Cher gracefully glided forward, her hair flowing in perfect rhythm to the rippling of her silky form-fitting floor-length gown as she towered over Sonny by six inches. She seemed to be a perfect mixture of Morticia Addams and Joan Baez, possessing beauty, strength, mystery, and a killer voice.

Each Tuesday night I felt a rush as the beauty swished her black shiny hair back over each slender shoulder. With every set change, her wardrobe became tighter and more revealing. Nothing could have pulled me out of my trance as I sat fixated on that sixteen-inch screen wishing 9:00 pm and the end of another evening with Cher would never come. I had no words for what I was feeling; all I knew was Tuesday was my favorite day of the week.

While most Americans were enjoying this new phenomenon, my household was caught between enjoyment and guilt. My parents, Don and Mary, had just joined a conservative, fundamentalist Baptist church, but they weren't sure yet how they felt about all the rules and opinions the church imposed on members. As regular attendees, they had found out quickly that Baptists did not make a habit of watching *The Sonny & Cher Comedy Hour*, having been told by pastors that it went too far in the direction of the pot-smoking sit-in folks we were seeing in the news. If we accepted such behavior on television, they said, it would be the beginning of the end for our morals. There might have been some truth in those statements, but there was no denying that *The Sonny & Cher Comedy Hour* gave me an important piece of information about myself that would take me quite some time to digest. Like most thirteen-year-olds at the time, I was not thinking about my sexual orientation. All I remember thinking was wow!

Still, I kept everything I was feeling to myself. I certainly did not want my parents to think I was being lured by the show's sensual content, knowing that if I expressed too much excitement about the show they would turn it off. I realized that for me Cher was the real attraction, and, although the word *homosexual* had never been used in our house, somehow I instinctively knew that being attracted to someone of the same sex was viewed as seriously wrong. Although I knew I could not confess my feelings, nothing about this attraction seemed strange to me. On the contrary, I felt only mind-blowing excitement. Most adolescents have felt a similar rush—if not for Cher, then for the Beatles, Greg Brady, Farrah Fawcett, Justin Bieber, or Katy Perry. It is a star-struck giddy excitement that makes eyes pop, hearts race, the adrenaline flow, and dreams of meeting them rush through the head. The thrill that comes naturally to any young boy in his room or any screaming dreamy-eyed girl at a concert is just as innate to gay people.

While my friends spoke endlessly about their latest boy crushes, I kept silent about my passion for the high-fashion pop star with the killer voice. Upon seeing pictures of male celebrities plastered on their bedroom walls, I tried to play along but could never muster up desire for the boys who held them captive. As my friends swooned over David Cassidy on the Partridge Family poster, my eyes took in the beautiful windblown silky hair of Susan Dey, right beside him. I was not trying to be different and yet I knew I *was* different.

CHAPTER 2

Home, Faith, and the Revelation at Church Camp

THE CONFLICT BETWEEN MY SEXUAL ORIENTATION and my commitment to God began in my early years of attending church camp, although at the time I lacked the awareness to express it clearly. My focus on Christianity started with my family's devotion to church. My parents, Methodist by birth, later switched to a Baptist church that eventually formed the basis for my own faith.

My father, like most boys born in the 1920s, was a child during the Great Depression then a man on the battlefields of World War II. As American patriotism swelled, my mother also joined the war effort, choosing nursing to aid the wounded. Before the war, they had lived in a small world, growing up in the same town and going to the same church. According to my mom's reminiscences, she didn't particularly care for my father initially, believing that he liked himself too much. But that all changed when he returned home from the war and she got a glimpse of him in his air force uniform. They married on the fifth anniversary of the attack on Pearl Harbor, December 7, 1946. Although their relationship was solid, many an anniversary we laughed over the same joke my mom would tell about December 7, the date two great wars started.

My parents gave very little thought to planning the births of their children. When we showed up, they were happy and just hoped they could somehow pay for another mouth to feed. My brother came along within fifteen months of their marriage, while my sister took a while to follow. Four years and twenty-three days after their wedding they had a boy and a girl. My father got a stable, decent-paying job at the telephone company, and my mom stayed at home. But when Philadelphia began its postwar suburban sprawl, my parents left their comfort zone for another world. Money from the GI Bill had helped them build a house eight miles from their childhood homes yet a world away from everything they had known. Like thousands of other young couples with dreams, they then left the city for the woods and cornfields of what was called suburban life, becoming a postwar perfect American family.

I imagine life was good during the eleven years before I arrived as a surprise. My parents must have eventually gotten used to the idea of having another child later in life because I never doubted that they loved me and were glad I came along. Of course, there were some adjustments. For instance, our ranch house was renovated into a raised cape to add more space as we were now the perfect Amercian family plus one.

We were not an especially close family. The age range of the children must have been a contributing factor. The age gap was so great that my brother, Russ, entered his first year of college as I began second grade. He was so much older than I that he seemed more like a stranger who came home only to eat, shower, and regroup for his next departure. I often thought of him as more of a visiting uncle I loved but didn't really know. Since Russ was a teenager by the time I reached the age of awareness, his participation in my life was minimal. By the time I was five, he was off having fun, playing sports, and participating in other typical teen activities. His life, unlike mine, followed the accustomed course: he finished college in four years with a degree in health and physical education, and then married and moved away, ready to face the future independently.

To my sister, Joyce, I was like a beloved pet. She would show me off as if I were a prize she had won at the fair, or a show-and-tell object brought from home. Even though I had been an accident, the six-year age difference between us allowed us to have the type of sibling relationship many people crave. We were not so close in age that a rivalry developed, but we were not so far apart that we went our separate ways. We seldom fought, instead forging a bond that grew strong and deep. I was her little sister prize, and she was my big sister source of joy.

My father, not unlike my Ken doll, was mostly silent. I saw him as handsome, and remember the ladies looking up at him and giggling the way women do when they are trying to make a man think what he just said was outrageously funny. He was six-foot-two, with a strong, sturdy torso; a barrel chest; black wavy hair that eventually turned a distinguished gray at the temples; dark blue eyes; and nicely shaped teeth. Even though he did not talk much, he had many interests; softball, gardening, and constant puttering kept him sufficiently busy. Like most men brought up in an English tradition, his affection was to be understood but not shared verbally or physically. An awkward kiss or a hug that was just a bit too hard was the most he could offer. As a child, I did not notice his subdued ways. I would throw myself at his large, robust frame with all the love my chubby little body could muster. Although he was always a reserved gentleman, I could tell that my affection toward him made him overjoyed yet befuddled. I believe he did want to let go of his heart and show how he felt toward me with reckless abandon but wasn't quite sure how to do it.

My mother, a study in complex oxymorons, was a combination of funny and fearful. She never minded laughing at herself and yet would panic to the point of paralysis at the realization that she had gotten lost on some road close to home. She had a fun, devil-may-care attitude, a quick wink, and was sure the worst that could happen would happen to her. She was a mother loved for her twinkling Irish smile and yet a woman riddled with anxiety. She was the best storyteller in the neighborhood, making my friends squeal with laughter, and yet a woman who kept her home as a members-only family fortress.

We were not much different from the other families on the block, but we did seem more likely to dress up and head to church each Sunday. Some of my earliest memories were of the beautiful, stately brick Methodist church that was my parents' spiritual home, though as time went on, they became increasingly concerned about the direction of the sermons. The sermons, instead of being based on Bible passages, were based more on what was happening in the news or on tips for childrearing from the latest *Ladies Home Journal*. When my sister came home at the age of eight and told my mother that she didn't learn any Bible stories in Sunday School, my parents agreed it was time to provide a more fulfilling spiritual life for their family.

The newly established Baptist church around the corner became our lasting spiritual home that set the stage for my later church affiliations. It was a Bible-believing, independent, fundamentalist, evangelical Baptist church with many taboos, including no dancing, no card playing, and no alcohol consumption.

As a Baptist child, I was instilled with an unwavering confidence that the Bible was the infallible word of God and that every word was correct and could be relied on for spiritual truth and everyday wisdom. I was taught that the Bible was the written expression of an all-powerful God reaching down to his creation and that the message of the scriptures was a powerful force for changing the world. Baptists originated when, in the early 1600s, a group of Christians separated from the Puritans, who had separated from the Catholics. The Baptists asserted that it was the Bible, not the organized Christian church, that should be the authority for spiritual instruction. They believed the church of the early 1600s, in an attempt to gain power and wealth, had polluted the original intent of the scriptures. These dissenters also became associated with baptizing in its original form, full immersion rather than sprinkling water on people. The word *baptism* in Greek means to immerse. The baptism ceremony—being submerged in water and then raised up again to start a new life—is symbolic of the death, burial, and resurrection of Jesus. With the act of baptism as their focus, another sect of Christianity was formed, which is today the fifth largest religious order on earth.

Our Baptist church was independent—that is, not affiliated with a larger church organization but rather self-governed, with a governing body made up exclusively of men who made decisions for the rest of the people. The fact that it was fundamentalist meant that it espoused the Five Fundamentals of the Faith: The Virgin Birth, The Trinity, The Infallible Word of God, The Forgiveness of Sin, and The Resurrection of Jesus from the Dead. The church was also evangelical, which meant that members were to tell others about the good news that the Five Fundamentals of the Faith were true and that we were loved by God and forgiven for our sins. Indeed, each fundamental of the faith formed the core and focus of my beliefs.

When I was six years old, my mother signed me up for a children's Bible club at the church. It turned out to be great fun, packed with games, Bible memorization, and singing. The teacher explained to us how we could be forgiven by God. At the time, I had never considered the need for forgiveness and yet I was certain I had told a few lies and occasionally been disobedient. Therefore I knew, when it was offered, that I needed forgiveness, already sensing that guilt separated me from a perfect God. The offer of forgiveness was freeing, joyous news that Jesus wanted to be my friend. To this day, I remember the jubilance I felt at being told that, while we were sinners, Christ had died for us and offered us forgiveness and unconditional love (Romans 5:8). This "good news," the starting point of every Christian journey, was the beginning of my personal spiritual life.

God was now real to me and a part of my daily existence. As a family, our lives were centered on the church. We had four opportunities every

Sunday to learn and worship—Sunday morning Sunday School for children and adults, Sunday morning worship service or Junior Church, Sunday late afternoon Jet Cadets; and Sunday evening service. In addition, there were midweek church gatherings on Wednesday nights, designed to refill the spiritual well. Wednesdays might have meant prayer and quiet time for the adults, but for me they meant Kid's Club, making Wednesday the best day of the week.

Kid's Club met in a long, wide basement room that mirrored the sanctuary above with cream-colored walls and 1950s tan and brown dash-patterned linoleum floors. The room could be sectioned off from the rest of the basement by pulling together two giant accordion doors—something only grown-ups had the strength to do. Listening to the rhythm of the mammoth doors as they clicked and swooshed over the gleaming tiles became a weekly ritual. Tucked safely inside, we prayed, we played, and we learned.

Kid's Club was like Girl Scouts with a Christian flair, including activities such as camping and crafts, in which it was possible to earn badges, with some Bible study thrown in. It felt like I was in my glory, being with girls all the time. I didn't have an explanation or true understanding of the reason for this, but I felt comfortable being in a world run by women. I earned so many badges that I needed to use the reverse side of my sash to display them—badges in archery, sewing, acting, baking, riflery, public speaking, fire building, horseback riding, swimming, and canoeing. And as I achieved I learned.

As I became adept at many activities, I grew in confidence and gained leadership skills. I was beginning to understand the Bible verse that says we can do "all things through Christ who strengthens us" (Philippians 4:13). I felt like I could conquer anything and make a difference in the world. The Bible verses I learned made sense and became a reflection of the way I lived my life, as well as the filter through which I viewed everyday events. God became my focus, and I wanted to live for him not just on Sundays and Wednesdays but every day, maybe eventually even in some full-time calling. I was young, but I was sure that God had something special planned for me, although I wasn't certain what it might be.

Even though Wednesday nights were my times to shine, they didn't come close to summer camp, a place where there were special moments every day that would bless me with a lifetime of memories. There the beauty of nature was intertwined with playful fun in the presence of God, who had created it all. Everywhere I went in the hundreds of acres that comprised the camp location, I was surrounded by groves of pine trees that enveloped me with intoxicating scents. Every step I took was softened by a blanket of their freshly dropped needles. The chilly morning dampness of the mountain above made me reluctant to crawl out of my sleeping bag, but the promise of another day in this sanctuary drew me from my warm cocoon. Campers played hard all day and met at campfire each evening. It was a place where God was spoken about freely at flag raising and each night before bed. The nonstop activities prevented me from getting homesick. By my second summer, one week in this paradise was not enough, and I begged my parents to allow me to go two then three weeks, and eventually a month each summer.

Camp was a spiritual high and brought further revelation of my sexual identity. It was there, at age eleven, that I began to realize I was attracted to strong women. I don't know a lesbian who wouldn't agree. They can be strong physically, like athletes, or they can be strong in confidence—it doesn't seem to matter. Either way we are uncontrollably attracted.

Strong women make our hearts pound and the corners of our mouths turn up with knowing smirks. My mouth first curled with such a smirk one morning at breakfast during my third summer at camp. Sometime between saying grace and passing the scrambled eggs, the heavy white commercial-sized door with its six-inch brass hinges swung wide, and a woman emerged from the kitchen. All six-foot-two, 180 pounds of her filled the rectangular opening as the banging pots and steam from the kitchen announced her entrance. She was big, she was strong, and there were rumors she could shoot a rattler between the eyes at a hundred yards. I did my best throughout the week to find reasons to stand outside below the kitchen windows to catch another glimpse of her. I wanted to talk to her, but it never happened. At the end of the week, I headed home with my parents to a world far away from my large, strong object of affection. All I knew was that she made me feel something strange and scary and wonderful. She didn't have any idea of the effect she had had on the little girl at table three. Without so much as a single gaze in my direction, she had started me down the path of a lifetime of smirking.

I didn't know where the smirk came from, nor did I comprehend its significance. But somehow I knew it was linked to something that was against the rules, and that made it all the more appealing. Something had begun; I just didn't have a name for it, and I was too immature to grasp the seriousness of the matter.

CHAPTER 3

Glory Days

SOFTBALL DID NOT MAKE ME A LESBIAN. But softball did bring together the qualities of strength and power in the sensuous heat of the summer, attracting me to the sport and increasing my awareness of having a different sexual orientation than my peers. Of course, not all women who play softball bat from the other side of the plate, but there are plenty of us.

My father started teaching me how to throw a softball when I was seven. An influential coach in our township leagues, he had started coaching years earlier with my brother's team. The passion he had toward the sport was infectious, and practice was a nightly ritual when the weather permitted. His drills were tough, designed not for a seven-year-old but more for someone aiming at playing in a major league. A typical evening would include a lengthy practice of catch followed by training in the proper technique of fielding dozens of grounders and pop flies. I remember crying when the ball careened off my chest or arm and my mom yelling at him to lighten up, which he did at least until the next night.

I started playing in a township league the summer before I entered third grade. Very uncharacteristically of my Baptist parents, my dad pulled a few strings and got me in under age. I spent my early years of softball moving from one position to another—pitcher, shortstop, and finally second base. Batting seemed to be my strength. With a couple of extra pounds and a lot of practice, I could be counted on for turning things around when the score wasn't in our favor. A softball can do damage, but to us the bumps and bruises were badges of courage. We could not possibly be playing hard enough, we figured, if a season went by without experiencing an incoming missile colliding with our leg or arm and imprinting its thread marks in a deep bruise. The girls who played routinely became the true athletes destined for high school teams. I was never the best player on my team, but all the practice paid off, encouraging me to keep playing year after year.

My dad introduced me to softball, but what kept me playing was the power, grace, and glory of the game. There was something in the dirt on a hot summer night; the way it got in your nose, your throat; the way it coated your fingers, your glove, your shoes; the way your glove felt, the sweat of it against your palm, the smell of the leather against your cheek; the fit of a new glove oiled and worked with your hands until it became a precise extension of your grasp; the feel of the power that pulsed through your arms as you gripped the bat and stared down the pitcher; the flexing of your forearms and the fine lines of your biceps as you taunted the field with the guessing game of where the ball might land; the power of the throw; the grace and fluid movement of the catch and tag; the force flowing through your body; the strength of your thighs as you propelled yourself around the bases. All of this led to the crescendo, the mad dash to glory.

I believe that most lesbians who play any sport would agree that there is a magical quality in the mingling of the senses and strength of our own bodies and the strength of our teammates that attracts us to sports. The appeal of mastering a skill and being able to not only play but win, proving the opposing team powerless, is at the heart of the attraction. Strong women bonded by playing powerfully together as a team is the major draw for lesbians engaged in sports. All these aspects, especially the lure of strength and power, fascinated me as I experienced newfound glory under the lights.

CHAPTER 4

Facing Conformity and Conflict

THOUGH WE NEVER SPOKE OF HER EXAMPLE, it was my mother who taught me how to face personal and spiritual conflicts. The idea, it seemed, was never to settle or obey rules out of blind obedience, but to stay true to one's personal convictions. From early childhood through high school, as I struggled with issues involving conformity I applied these lessons in conflict resolution that I had learned from my mother despite her weaknesses.

As a child, although I was busy with church, camp, and softball I experienced loneliness. Of the few children in the neighborhood who were my age, none seemed to escape my mother's blacklist, her compilation of people too flawed to associate with me without causing me harm. I was not encouraged to "go out and play"; consequently, summer days were often spent in the company of my mother and her women friends. Good and bad came from this arrangement. As I spent time with my mother's women friends, my vocabulary and social skills improved beyond my years, easing my social interactions with adults. However, I never felt like I had a real childhood. My mother's friends were always kind and jovial toward me, never making me feel unwanted or bothersome. They listened to me, laughed at my antics, and treated me as part of their everyday world. It was as if I were a smaller version of the other women in the group, making me once again at home in a world run by women.

During junior high school, my conflicting feelings about my sexual orientation intensified. I felt like an outsider peering into the lives of others around me and, unable to muster the relevant feelings, had no idea how to get in. I endured a pudgy puberty, feeling like the Stay Puft Marshmallow Man. I also spent three years riding on the end of my personal emotional pendulum, which was in perpetual motion. I could easily swing from being in ecstasy over the latest 45 record to hit the charts to, moments later, being in agony over the fact that my mother could not possibly know about the woes of a young teenager. I did my best to chase boys, as I thought I was supposed to do, but never seemed to be boy crazy like my friends. My interest in boys came instead from my attempt to fit in rather than from any feeling that came naturally. I told myself that I was normal, but I sensed that maybe I was missing something. With each new boyfriend, the initial thrill would subside and a feeling of flatness would creep in. I would attempt to feel the euphoria that my girlfriends had over their first dance or first kiss, yet emotionally there was nothing but a gray lifeless cloud. I thought I was doing what every other thirteen-year-old girl was doing, but while all my friends seemed happy I was just trying to survive.

These confused feelings were intensified when I was shown a hardcore nudie magazine by my peers. I had been hanging out after school with a new girlfriend who lived a few blocks away. My mother hadn't found out what was wrong with her yet, so I had been spared discussions about why I shouldn't be in this new girl's company. Maybe Mother should have been worried since the new girl's best buddies were the bad boys from the next neighborhood. One day five of us pedaled as fast as we could to the hiding place where they had stashed the goods the day before, near the delivery road at the side of a mall. The prize was hidden beneath the bushes that wrapped around and down the sides and top of a drainpipe in a twist of discarded trash and thorns. Magazine in hand, the boys hoisted themselves to their feet, holding the tattered pages carefully in wide-eyed reverence.

Standing silently in a circle, we passed around the pages of black-and-white photos, shredded as if they had been blown from one of the passing trucks. I felt dirty. I felt wrong. I felt confirmed. While the men's parts seemed an oddity, I could see nothing but beauty in the women's lovely round breasts. I acknowledged to myself that this was not right. I knew I was taking my time on the pages that revealed the women's bodies and then handing off quickly the pages containing pictures of the naked men. I did not meet the eyes of the others, fearing they would be able to read my thoughts. I had not lived my life up until then focused on, or fretting about, my sexuality, but now I could not ignore it. I wondered why I didn't find the men at least interesting, if not attractive. I initially told myself that having never seen the male nude body before, I was not attracted to it because I was unfamiliar with it.

I spent many days ashamed at what I had done. However, I spent many more days pondering the fact that looking at nude photos of men and women had confirmed for me something about my sexuality. But as quickly as my validation had come I dismissed it, saying to myself that when I fall in love with a man the love for those strange body parts would come. I consoled myself by thinking that I was just like every other woman trying to find her way.

For quite a while I set my sights on learning to conform rather than further acknowledging my different sexual identity. Having observed the social caste system around me, I concluded that I was supposed to find cute boys, flirt with them, get them to pursue me, be their girlfriend, and kiss them—or maybe even go a little further but not too far. Consequently, making out with boys became a self-appointed assignment. But although I began kissing boys a lot, there was a hollowness to my actions. And every attempt to engage in a relationship made it increasingly apparent to me that relationships based on conversation, understanding, and care were nonexistent.

I did not realize that there was complexity to this thing called love. While all the other girls seemed thrilled with the prospect of finding someone to call their own, I felt empty during such pursuits. And the more I dated, the farther away I knew I was from the feelings my girlfriends seemed to have. While my friends seemed to want "forever" with the boys they adored, not one of the boys I dated made me think of marriage or babies. To me, the boys were objects to obtain by the time of the homecoming dance or other important school events. The physical show of having a boyfriend was all I was ever able to achieve. I did not and could not seem to go any further toward what I later found out was love, and so increasingly gained certainty that I was different.

By the end of ninth grade, my weight had ballooned, and I knew it had to go so I could be part of the in-crowd upon entering high school months later. I spent the summer in Weight Watchers and watched the pounds melt week after week until I was nothing more than some well-placed curves.

Thirty pounds leaner, I tried out for our state's best field hockey team and made it. As an official member of the jocks, I was convinced I was on my way to popularity and fame. My love for softball had not waned, but field hockey was even better, like softball on steroids.

All the things I had loved about softball also applied to my new sport—strong women playing as a group on a powerful team. But the experience I remember most about field hockey was being warned about my behavior by a coach who seemingly cloaked her gayness in sternness and authority.

In general, warmth was not in our coach's repertoire. She never paid much attention to me, not once offering so much as a hello in the hallway—until the day, two years into my playing career, when, after practice, she summoned me for a conversation that would be a forerunner of other excruciating conversations I would later have with various authority figures concerning my sexual identity. When the coach called me to her office, a twenty-yard walk from the locker room, I did not have time to mull over possible reasons for her request. As she closed the door behind me, the assistant coach, seated at her desk, turned toward us as if preparing to listen to our meeting. The only light in the windowless office streamed from the reading lamp at each desk, providing an ominous atmosphere. The coach sat perched on the corner of her desk with a reading lamp illuminating her from behind, the circle of the beam framing the back of her head with a halo of light. Somehow I knew immediately that, despite her artificial angelic radiance, she would not be giving me glad tidings of great joy. In a stern tone, she released her words rapidly, like a hail of bullets from a machine gun spattering my body, mind, and heart with her painful pronouncement, saying, "Gilmore, you'd better watch how you act; you don't want anybody to think you are gay," as if being gay was the worst thing in the world. She might as well have said, "You don't want anybody to think you have leprosy, do you?" Her words shocked me, and I left the office without knowing if I had said anything in response. But as soon as I heard the door shut behind me and stepped into the hall, a grin spread from cheek to check. As the smile spread across my face, a realization spread within me, and for the first time, an answer came to me that I would never have dared to actually say to the coach: "But I *am* gay."

As I walked to the bus, my gait became a rhythmical drumbeat, each step accentuating a word of the refrain "But I-*Am*-Gay. But I-*Am*-Gay." The beat of my steps came from my sense of freedom at having experienced enlightenment. My reaction surprised me. I had not been frightened by her words or intimidated by her power. The experience had surprisingly been an opportunity for validation and courage. I was glad to know who I was, or who I was becoming.

Why the coach had felt the need to call me into her office to warn me in this manner was a mystery, but I had a theory. She was in her late forties and had experienced the climate in our state's schools supporting prejudice against gays and threats of firing gay teachers whose sexual orientation was discovered. Maybe she had seen me flirting with some of the players and, sensitive to bigotry from her own past experience, did not want me to be hurt. From the way she asked me to hide my identity, I surmised that she herself lived in fear as a gay middle-aged woman and had to deny her sexual orientation. I did not know her circumstances, but it seemed to me that her statement could only have come from another gay person who had experienced a lifetime of hurt. Since she was my coach, however, I could not ask her the questions I had. As for me, I knew that secrecy and denial would lead to heartache and fear and thus I could not keep that generation's expectations. I could not allow my heart to shrivel in my chest. I would need to find a way to be brave amidst the mores of the current society. I would have to find a way to be true to myself.

My spirit of rebellion and soul-searching about my sexual identity was maintained with the arrival of the women's movement. Women five and ten years my senior began burning their bras and becoming self-actualized. The world seemed open to endless possibilities. The thought of equality in the workplace and in other areas of society resonated with me. My favorite courses in high school were English, social studies, and especially women's studies, where we learned about the strong women who pioneered causes and changed history, including those in the suffrage movement and those who demanded equal pay for equal jobs. I was particularly struck by the concept that radicalism was required for change, that most of the positive change in women's rights had come from daring women who had not only pushed the envelope but forced it open with wildly new ideas, altering the way women were treated and promising lasting change for the future.

However, on Sundays I still heard a much different message when my church leadership spoke of the place of women in society, saying they were equal in the mind of Christ but that their role was to be submissive to men. Further, the church asserted that women could only be in a leadership or teaching position with women and children. They were to obey their husbands as well as the male leadership of the church. I wondered how I could mesh these church views with my forming self-image bolstered by beliefs of the emerging women's movement? What would my future look like as a Bible believer who also thought that women were capable of playing a larger role in the church and community? I could only hope that the common sense of the women's movement would trickle down to the broader society and the church. I realized that the church needed to adhere to the teachings of the scriptures but felt there would eventually have to be reasonable compromise with regard to women's rights and permitted roles. While I knew it would be a long road to reach such compromises, perhaps decades, I believed it would happen and would be worth the wait.

I felt that Susan B. Anthony and the women of the suffrage movement who worked to gain women the right to vote must have felt the same way, aware of the difficulties involved in persuading society to view women as being equally capable as men and therefore deserving equal rights. Yet they pushed on. The dream of women having equality in the workplace and equal pay must have also seemed impossible to Gloria Steinem, and yet she persisted. I admired these bold, radical pioneers, and I never forgot how their dreams and actions made a difference in changing society. The women's movement opened my eyes to the reality that one person can help change the world. I knew I was willing and able; I just didn't yet know the cause I would be called to fight.

High school was a time of discovering that all students were feeling their way toward their authentic selves and that my mother had her own conflicts regarding her fundamentalist Baptist faith and her private beliefs and behavior. She had no problem abstaining from alcohol since she'd never had any in the first place. She had no problem not smoking either. She had even given up playing cards with her women friends. But she could not give up dancing, as music touched her soul. According to anyone at church who knew of the error of her ways, she was a living rebel. She would conform only to a degree and on her own terms. Whatever she would do, she would do it because it was right, making decisions that considered not only the God of the Bible but also the peace of her soul. While the other teens from church stayed home from the school dances, my mother helped me select my outfits for the evenings. The lesson was loud and clear: there were conflicting beliefs in our family regarding the dogma of the Baptist church and the life-affirming exuberance of dancing. We were Baptists with the boogie-woogie blues.

Most of my mother's conflicts were resolved quickly, some with an easy surrender, some with quiet rebellion. To her, God's word was to be followed, but the extra list of dos and don'ts did not need to be considered sacred. If the Bible was not clear on a subject, an action was not mandatory but open to decision based on conscience. Among other churchgoers this attitude was seen as rebellion. But to me it was a wonderful acknowledgment of the freedom we have as Christians. It made me proud to know my mother lived her life making conscious decisions about her conduct. Her example encouraged me to think. Even though in high school I already knew that the conflict I would face about my sexual identity would be more significant than any my mother had encountered, I sensed that I would ultimately follow her example, adhering to God's word but considering the extra dos and don'ts of church dogma not as mandatory but as decisions to be made according to conscience. I would let the God of the Bible be the one to inform my conduct and bring peace to my soul.

CHAPTER 5

All In for God

THE SALVATION OF MY HIGH SCHOOL YEARS was my high school nights. Our church's teens joined with teens from a neighboring church to form a youth group that became the light of my existence. Two hundred cool kids strong, it was the "in" place to hang. As a large group of enthusiastic high school kids wanting God to be a bigger part of their lives, it was groundbreaking at the time. We did everything from taking trips to the beach to attending car rallies and concerts, activities that left me with fantastic memories. It met my needs like nothing else I had experienced and nurtured development of my skills and knowledge.

The youth pastors were young and vibrant. Their ministry style was cutting edge, far from the hymn-singing and staid religious practices of my youth. Their lives demonstrated their passion for God's work. Their speaking abilities drew me in as I hung on every word. Within months, it became clear that this type of ministry to youth was something that resonated with me and matched my talents. My leadership abilities came forward, and my Bible knowledge was called on to facilitate some of the studies. As a result, I discovered it could actually be fun to serve the God I loved and I was ready to pursue an education to prepare for spiritual service.

In the years prior, I had been on a much different career path. I thought I would follow my brother's choice and train to be a physical education teacher and perhaps minor in political science. I had been accepted at a few schools with that goal in mind, but these plans quickly faded. The thought of having Christian ministry as my life's work made my soul rejoice, and I could think of no better way to spend my life than to serve God by leading others to him. My mother was thrilled at the idea of having a Christian worker in the family. My father was not so sure, wondering if I would be able to make a living in such a career. But money did not matter to me; I was sure my plans would take me exactly where God wanted me to be.

Since both youth pastors at our church had graduated from the same Bible college, I was sure that was where I wanted to get my training. So while others around me struggled to decide their future, I applied to Florida Bible College and was accepted. I was at peace. Though I wondered sometimes about how my sexual orientation would impact my career choice, I was not going to let my sexuality stand in my way. I was certain that if God wanted me to be in the Christian ministry, he would create a way for me to fall in love with a wonderful guy. I trusted that he would surely transform me into the woman he wanted me to be.

While waiting for this next phase of my life to begin, I spent much of my spare time in a Christian-type rock band of eight individuals. Rock and roll had invaded our culture, and we loved it, but our fundamentalist Baptist church leaders were not too sure. Rock and roll had always been described as "Satan's music," "of the Devil," "the beat of sexual temptation." Thus, while the teens around us were rocking out to Jethro Tull and Peter Frampton our rock and roll included a little swaying and maybe even some clapping. Our group didn't have the ear-piercing metal sounds of the electric guitar, the feet stomping, hair-flying movements of rock stars, or the grungy rock group couture. The girls' outfits of our rock band were conservative, baby blue floor-length polyester gowns. Nevertheless, we thought we were on the cutting edge of the fundamentalist church scene of the 1970s. We were trying to introduce new music to a culture whose latest popular tune had been written in the 1800s. The instrumentalists were solid; we had no standout vocalists. My part was first soprano. Tull and Frampton evoked fan hysteria; our old recordings brought a whole new meaning to the word *hysteria*.

Maybe with a little vision and some better singers we could have gone farther. Instead, our audiences were restricted to the congregations of several churches. We were well received by the under-forty crowd, while the elders did their best to politely welcome us. Despite the racket that we called music, these elders were just glad to see young people still coming to church. Even with all our swaying and corniness, I was proud to be part of such a group during this era, and I still believe we made a difference. We were one band among many that added beat to Christian music and helped introduce contemporary music to the church of the 1970s.

Although the band also served the function of keeping me busy and focused on my future in the Christian ministry, with my teen hormones raging, not even the constant practices and evenings with my church friends could keep me from continuing on the quest for my sexual identity. In fact, during these years before college I led a life of hypocritical double standards that were against my faith and against all reason. My sexual exploitations were first and foremost contrary to my Christian faith. The Bible teaches us to be sexually pure before marriage, to be monogamous; I was neither. I had a boyfriend and a girlfriend, too. She knew about him, but he did not know about her. It was all so ungodly, so unscrupulous—and so exciting. I also had a double standard for my sexual activity. While I never thought of going all the way with my boyfriend, my escapades with my girlfriend knew no bounds. A big factor was the threat of pregnancy. With that risk eliminated, the green light was on, and the flags were waving.

My boyfriend was a wonderful human being, fun, but also the stable type with a good future ahead. We kissed; we went a bit further. But there was a looming problem. No matter how many months we dated, even though I felt the special excitement of having a boyfriend the next step to deeper intimacy seemed like reaching into a fog unable to see what it engulfed, while being pretty sure that I would not be satisfied with what I might find. I did not struggle with the physical aspect, as some lesbians do; it was the giving of my whole heart that was impossible.

While in high school, I did not take what I was doing seriously. I was sure the white hot nights spent with my auburn-haired girlfriend would be replaced with a marriage to some nice guy with whom I would have children. But my sense of a looming problem was gradually digging a circular trench around my conscious mind. The thought of not being able to love a man brought panic as it leaped to the forefront of my thinking, only to be pushed aside until it haunted me once again. The fact was that the idea of a life spent attempting to love a man sounded absolutely boring to me. I had tasted young real love, the kind of love that makes you want to give all and share all with another human being, and it had not been with Mister Right. Undeniably, I was in love with an auburn-haired teenage girl. For now, there seemed to be a wall that kept me from wanting to give my love to a male. All I knew was that with the auburn-haired girl I built bridges I could run across. With my boyfriend, I made excuses, and the wall seemed to grow higher. Despite this, I tried to assure myself that all would be well when I found the right man and it was time to settle down.

Fortunately, the church had given me direction for my future. The rock band had offered me a sense of belonging. The auburn-haired girl had shown me the heat of young love. The fact that I was simultaneously experiencing all these aspects of myself that were so disparate should have been my clue about the danger that lay ahead.

CHAPTER 6

Being Held in God's Hand

WHILE MY YOUTH GROUP HAD GIVEN ME a sense of direction for a future in the ministry, the sudden death of my father provided me with unshakable certainty of God's existence and love, especially in times of trouble. This event also forced me to review my relationship with my father and his relationship with others in the community. Although my dad was most often quiet, serious, and reserved, during my childhood I never stopped pursuing his affection, and I remember receiving it in small but meaningful ways.

Sundays were when he was most apt to bring me into his world. When I was a young child, he would stand me up on the toilet lid so I could watch him shave his bristly face in the mirror on the opposite wall. He would sing to me and teach me silly songs and hymns, and I learned to sing along. "Jimmy Crack Corn and I Don't Care," "In the Garden," and "The Old Rugged Cross" were his favorites. My favorite, which I would beg him to sing again and again, was a song about Henry the Eighth's wife Anne Boleyn, who was beheaded at the Tower of London—certainly not a tune you'd think a young girl would like. While singing the dark, gloomy chorus, my father would put his elbow up around his face and stalk toward me chanting, "With her head tucked underneath her arm . . . she walked the bloody tower." These episodes were frightening but also endearing. The song made my dad real, causing him to drop his guard and expose his soft side that I longed to connect with. The Sunday morning ritual continued throughout our two-block walk to church. I would reach for his hand, which he offered freely, but my tiny hand could not hold his comfortably. So hand in thumb we would walk to our favorite place. I felt safe and happy to be his little girl.

On other days I would often wait at the corner where he was usually dropped off by a buddy on his way home from work. We would walk the short block together, and I would announce his arrival to my mother as I burst through the front door. With my brother and sister away pursuing their young adult lives, the three of us would sit down to dinner at precisely 5:30, an all-American family of three.

While my brother was off at college and my sister was involved in teenage activities, my dad and I would work on projects around the house together, he the handyman and I the adoring gopher. I learned to be quiet and stand by for my next order. When the day was over, we would watch television together, lying on the floor, and even on the hottest summer nights I would ignore the heat and snuggle close to him.

In considering whether my relationship with my father gave me any indication of my sexual orientation, I believed it did—if I had known of the possibility then. Although my father was tall and handsome, even at an early age I found myself more often repelled by his physique than drawn to his beauty. I loved him, but his body hair and musky odor did more to turn me away than to draw me toward him. There seemed to always be an invisible wall between us, built from his side by his seeming inability to show affection and from my side by a force that told me the love of a man was not what I was looking for.

Besides our Sunday and weekday routines, other highlights of our time together were the holidays. My family did its best to raise the American stress level over Christmas to new heights. For some reason, my father would take the week preceding Christmas off.

In theory it sounded like a nice thing to do—to help his wife with the last-minute preparations of shopping, wrapping, cookie baking, and tree decorating. But instead of helping out with Christmas, my father would use this week to begin new projects around the house. The whole idea of starting something new this week, ripping the house apart as guests would be arriving, was considered insane by all the occupants of the house except my father, who thought it was a fine idea. About fifteen minutes after he awoke the first Monday home, he would begin his first chosen task, and, like clockwork, fifteen minutes later the yelling would begin. My mother, whose temperament was like an erupting volcano from Thanksgiving until after Christmas, was always the first to voice her opinion. Her volume did not begin softly and grow louder; instead, it started at ear-splitting decibels fueled by frustration as she shrieked, "Don, is that absolutely necessary? Why can't you help me with something that we actually need to do?" From there he did as much as he could to just stay out of the way. The yard, basement, and garage were his safe havens. Even though I often sided with my father during my mother's tirades, I can remember thinking that she had a point. Eventually, when Christmas Day arrived at our house it was great; we just had to be sure to live through the previous week.

Christmas week held the rush of anticipation with last-minute good behavior in case elves were watching, focusing on the decorating of the Christmas tree. In our house, the atmosphere was not one of hot cocoa drinking and carol singing. Instead, an atmosphere prevailed that was a combination of my mother's neurosis and my father's long suffering, with me feeling disappointed.

For some reason, my mother would not allow us to have a Christmas tree on the floor. I don't know if she was afraid of ruining the hardwood floors with the leaking stand or if they were both too cheap to spring for a taller tree. But I remember our tree being placed on top of a ratty-looking card table that was shoved into a corner in the living room. This live tree not only had been plucked from the earth before its time, but a rope was wrapped around the top of it and anchored by nails to the windowsills. When it was standing like a tree in submission, my father and I would trim it, laughing together as we placed all the handmade ornaments and family heirlooms in their appointed places, making it look beautiful—that is, until my mother came for an inspection. For my mother, there were never enough ornaments, never enough tinsel. By the time she got done with her trimming, it was impossible to tell what was beneath the decorations. Each year, the infant tree in bondage overloaded with Christmas trimmings was the center of our holiday world.

As the years passed, my brother finished college, married, moved a few hours away, and started a family. My sister also married but remained in the area. Alone with my parents, my feelings of being an only child became an acute reality.

When I was sixteen, my dad died suddenly at age fifty-three, which was an earth-shattering experience for me. It is said that it's a shock no matter how your loved ones go, but in our little world Dad's means of death measured on the Richter scale. My dad was the type to stay in shape, still playing softball with the young guys and volleyball on the township leagues. Usually the picture of health, the day of his death he called in to work sick, complaining about a severe pain in his abdomen. If it really hurt that bad, it was not clear why he didn't go to the emergency room or to a doctor. After one day of feeling sick, he went into convulsions and died on our living room floor, with my mother and me trying desperately to save him. To this day, the precise cause of his death is a mystery. When we saw the results of the autopsy, they told us that his heart had been healthy but his spleen was enlarged two or three times the normal size and his white blood count was very high.

My father's funeral was sad, somber, but most of all, eye-opening. My quiet dad—who had hung back in a crowd and seemed to always want to be an assistant instead of a leader, who never talked about what was happening at work, and who seemed not to want to do more than putter in his garden—had six hundred people at his funeral. My sister, brother, and I stood awkwardly in the reception line as condolences were whispered by unfamiliar people who had been touched by his life, saying such things as "the life of the party," "ever giving, ever sharing," "kind to us when we needed help," "a true leader." As my sister, brother, and I marveled, our expressions of sympathy turned to each other. "I am so sorry," I told my brother. "I know how close you were to him." And my brother replied, "No, not really. I thought you were closest to him." The evening and the following days brought many more questions than answers about our dad's identity. We had loved him, but it was the rest of the world that told us about the surprising legacy of our silent father.

God had taken my father, and I knew beyond a doubt that he was with God and happy. My father had been a Christ follower; his early morning Bible reading had been an inspiration to me for years. But even with my faith a deep grief hovered over my life for more than a year after his death. I followed my normal routine—school, sports, youth group—but the deepest part of me was not fully present. My first waking thoughts were clouded with a foreboding sense of loss. Feeling comfortless and unable to rise from the despair, I never knew what circumstance would take my breath away or restart my tears. Having a dull ache in my chest became a familiar feeling in my anatomy. But again and again it was the memories of small hallowed moments that sent me to my knees: waking up on a weekday thinking I had heard my dad in the kitchen making my breakfast; certain of seeing him in a crowd and running toward him till I realized it just couldn't be; setting the table and grabbing three forks from the drawer when only two were needed.

But I felt I was right about God having a plan. I knew God wouldn't let me sink too deep in despondency but would reach down and prove that he cared. One evening I experienced just this: an encounter with a spiritual being who gave me relief from depression. I am unsure if it took the form of a ministering angel, Jesus, or energy from the Holy Spirit, but I do know unshakably that, because of what I experienced, there is a God in heaven who loves and who cares.

I was lying face down on my bed in a state of overwhelming sorrow, crying and muttering a prayer. Then I suddenly felt peace. The feeling started as a feather-light but firm pressure on my chest, soon covering the rest of me like a giant warm hand. Within a moment, the hand was holding me—body, mind, and soul. I felt like I was in God's hand and he was reminding me of his love and protection. The peace I felt was transforming, settling the turmoil in my soul. I drifted off into a paradise, asleep in the hand of God. The next morning I woke with renewed faith and certainty about God's existence and love. I realized that none of us can escape the cruelties of life but all of us can ask to be held by the hand of God and find peace.

CHAPTER 7

Making a Break for Independence

THE TIME BETWEEN THE DEATH OF MY FATHER and departing for college was spent breaking bonds of fears and emotional ties to win increased independence. Now I was living alone with my mother, which meant living with her fears. It also meant being the go-to person when each new presumed tragedy reared its irrational head. For example, any solo car travel she attempted outside the area prompted intense fear of getting lost. As this was long before the days of cell phones, she would find a roadside phone booth and call me, having already worked herself into a frenzy for fear that she would never find her way home. Roads she had tried kept leading her in circles. Exit ramps were bypassed because she was not sure where they would lead her. Pleading and sobbing conversation would always end with her saying, "You need to come get me." Even if I was in the middle of a softball game or out for the evening with friends, I would go because she needed me.

Regarding her fear of illness, Webster could have used my mother's photograph under his definition of hypochondria. She always either had some exotic disease or was sure one would soon be entering her body to render her blind or spotted or mad. Her medical training had given her just enough knowledge to imagine numerous potentially dangerous conditions—liver flukes, surgical instruments left behind.

She also had a fear of decisions and ensuing action, once taking two years to pick out a living room chair only to be sure when it arrived that she had selected the wrong one. At the beginning of the chair-buying process, I had been excited about seeing something new in the house and encouraged her to make a selection. But before long I didn't care if the thing was orange and red plaid because my stomach hurt so much from the turmoil. At their worst, her fears paralyzed her from experiencing life to its fullest and challenged her faith since she could not let the God she loved help her overcome them. It was heartbreaking to see her not let him into the darkness that overtook her.

My mother's fears intensified our parent-child role reversal as well, which had deepened the minute my father died. Everyday problems became mine, and, while aware of how unhealthy the dynamic was, I determined that I was the one who had to be strong to keep us going.

Ultimately, my mother's fears catalyzed my own strength. Years of watching them take her further from her potential made me determined to be brave and courageous. Over and over again, I would tell myself to depend on God, that God had promised to watch over me, care for me, and give me strength. Time after time I would run to him—and time after time he would faithfully come to my aid, even when I almost buckled under the weight of my mother's neediness. Finally I vowed that I would not be afraid to drive somewhere new; not let sickness overwhelm my spirit; and, if there was a decision to be made, consider the options and move forward, remembering that accumulations of wasted energy formed regrets.

As my plans for going away to college gelled, I realized I had grown up wiping my mother's tears. I knew I would be going where God was telling me to go and my mother would have to become God's worry. But I had not yet figured out what to do with my serious boyfriend and the lovely auburn-haired girl.

It was hard not to love my wonderful, churchgoing boyfriend, who would make a good father one day. On the other hand, the auburn-haired beauty was the one who drew me. And although it was a taboo subject, the look in my mother's eye, and her constant questions about the excessive amount of time we spent together, made me sense that she knew there was much more to us than two girls in an average friendship. Yet I was certainly not going to tell her of my passion, and she was not going to ask, not wanting to face the truth. I was secretly glad I would not have to face my father when the truth would eventually be revealed. Although the specter of his disapproval of me flickered in and out of my mind, I did my best to dismiss foreboding thoughts about what would happen if and when my sexual orientation became undeniably apparent to my mother. Fortunately, my mother was not willing to turn to anyone with her suspicions. All she could do was hope that my inclination toward girls would be left behind as I departed for the faraway land of Florida.

My boyfriend was already in college, studying for successful employment. The problem was he did not have my heart. It was easy to make my decision. I was leaving in a few weeks, so I simply told him to go ahead and date others while I was gone. After a year and a half of dating, I had spoken from a place of cold complacency, never imagining that he might not feel the same way. In truth, I had projected my lack of feelings onto him and concluded he did not love me. I remember him shedding a tear, and it was over. Ignorantly heartless and selfish, I began a new life. I told myself I was on to bigger and better things, that my real man would be in Florida. What I was still missing was one hidden but crucial piece of information: I was not capable of fully loving any man.

The auburn-haired beauty was another story. I could not so easily accept her leaving my life. On the one hand, there was no room for a love affair with a woman in my vision of the future. On the other hand, I didn't know how to give up the fire and deep bond we shared. In the end, I believed the relationship was wrong. The future was calling, and the breakup had to happen. I would do my best to forget her.

College was calling. Like every other freshman, I was leaving loved ones behind. I left my mother alone to learn to push through her fears on her own. I left my boyfriend with permission to find someone new. I left the fire I had found in the arms of a woman, promising myself I would never again dabble in lady love. I shed the dramas of the past to discover a bright new future.

CHAPTER 8

Bible College and the Bluegrass Boy

I LEFT FOR BIBLE COLLEGE WITH THE FERVENT HOPE that God would show me what he wanted me to do with my life, and yet all I could think about was the adventure awaiting me in Florida. I arrived at Miami International Airport on August 22, 1976, at 10:00 pm. Even at that hour, the heat that met us as the stewardess opened the plane's exit door was like a wall of steaming hot washcloths. The van ride from the airport passed through streets lined with tropical palm trees still in the heavy night air, and hundreds of perfectly square short houses on perfectly square lots. Pink stucco glittered in the moonlight like a million tiny diamonds. As we turned on to the mile-long boulevard that connected Hollywood with the beach, ancient palms lined our path like welcoming sentinels standing in regal splendor. In the distance a massive hotel rose up from the beach, with a high central tower and arms that spread to the sides as if in a welcoming posture. As we pulled onto campus, I could not have been more impressed; the main structure shimmered like a magical jewel in the moonlight against the backdrop of the endless Atlantic Ocean. This was my new world, so different from anything I had previously experienced.

The hotel that now housed the Bible college had been erected in the 1930s as a resort and moneymaking enterprise for the infamous Al Capone. It was a masterpiece of modern engineering where, during its heyday, famous gangsters and the newly rich had mingled, gambling and dancing the nights away. But after the Great Depression hit and the beautiful ladies and handsome gents no longer made the long journey, the massive building had proved hard to maintain and slowly fell into disrepair. A depressed real estate market then created an opportunity for Florida Bible College to buy it. I was amused at the strange and ironic way God had worked to turn a hotel once used for all things we called taboo into a place for the teaching of God's word.

Traces of the structure's origins still lingered despite the building's new, more conservative function. There were at least two bars with curved red leather seats framed in stunning mahogany. There was also a mirrored ballroom with parquet flooring and crystal sconces that hung like tiny waterfalls from each pillar. Secret foldaway walls held paintings of scantily clad women who had no doubt entertained illegal poker players.

But despite the fact that such activities were taboo for the college students, our existence was far from austere. The newer portion of the college included a cafeteria with a forty-yard bank of windows overlooking the ocean. Our dorm rooms were the old hotel rooms, each with a private bath. Even though I was in a foreign location, I had never felt so at home. The joy, peace, and contentment I experienced led me to the conclusion that indeed I was where God wanted me to be. I felt alive, and was sure I was going to hit my stride as I studied in anticipation of a life of service.

Friendships came quickly, and with very little effort I was elected freshman class secretary. The positions of president and vice president were off limits to women as men were considered the leaders. To Bible colleges in the South, this policy was accepted as the natural order, in keeping with the scriptures. Even though my recent education in women's rights should have prompted me to protest, my mind allowed for compromise, settling somewhere between the truth of the scriptures and a reality with which I could live. The scriptures did teach that men were to be leaders at home and in the church, but I did not believe this leadership role carried over to all circumstances of life. I thought that women could be just as influential but had to find their own places of power within society.

I determined that the role of student council secretary would be my podium. At our school, those elected to student council were looked up to as spiritual leaders, elected because others in their class knew by their words and actions that they were leaders who loved God and wanted to make a difference in others' lives. I was honored that my peers had seen my potential. The responsibility of planning social events, leading Bible studies, and being involved in outreach programs filled my days with joy. God had put me in a place that fit me perfectly. With the boundless energy of a seventeen-year-old, I studied all day and socialized each evening.

At first, I phoned home to the auburn-haired girl often, missing her. There was an evident contrast between my feelings for the boy and the girl I had left behind. In just a few weeks, the boy had already receded into the distant past, but my feelings for the girl were still strong. As weeks passed and school quickly demanded my every waking hour, more time elapsed between phone calls, yet I could not stop calling. I needed to hear her voice. It was about love and desire. It was about having found the first person who made my heart skip a beat. In my position, it was lovely madness.

My studies went well, and each semester my grade point average was high. I didn't just learn; I devoured each book placed before me. Every class taught me the worth of the book I had come to study: the Bible. To study the Bible is to study history, the mind of God, the foibles of humankind, psychology, the most ancient wisdom known to human beings, and the plan of God and his intention for humankind and his creation. I had never been so enthralled with my studies, and I was at peace.

The plan of most students at the Bible college was to live a life of service. The men would be pastors, Christian education directors, youth pastors, or missionaries, and the women had to find positions assisting those roles. It was widely assumed, although rarely acknowledged, that the women could find their places of service by marrying men who would be church leaders.

From a broader perspective, all students understood that both men and women knew they would be more employable if they were married. Men needed wives before becoming pastors of churches as no church wanted a single man in the pulpit, believing he would be distracted looking for a wife or, worse, looking at women already involved in a relationship. Similarly, the women needed men to be effective in church service since we were only allowed service roles focused on the instruction and nurturing of the other women and children within the church. For women who found husbands destined to be pastors, employment and respect were certainties.

Awareness of this system caused me anxiety, but I believed it would all work out. I was sure that God, knowing of my desire to reach my full potential in serving him, would bring me my pastor-husband, the man I would love. And while waiting to find Mr. Right, I was determined not to let my anxiety about future possibilities get me down, remembering the Bible verse: "Seek first the kingdom of God, and all things will be added to you" (Luke 12:31). Consequently, I believed my job was to learn all I could and help others in any way possible around the college. Initially, I dated casually, but no knight came forward on a white horse bearing a diamond, and I did not go out of my way to attract one.

For now, I was content with my small group of friends, three guys and six girls who had arrived from six different northern and midwestern states, all wide-eyed with excitement. Punch drunk from our newfound independence, we lived life like most college freshman without, of course, drinking, attending wild parties, and having premarital sex. Along with studies, there was always some kind of low-budget activity to make us happy. We would go out for ice cream, down to the pier to watch the moon shimmering on the water, drive to Miami Beach to see the bright lights of the posh hotels that lined the water, or spend all day on a quest to get to Key West and back, just to say we did. My favorite activity was to go to the Fort Lauderdale airport, where we parked on a service road in the darkness and lay on our backs on the hood of the car, gazing up into the warm tropical night as we watched the incoming planes, their massive tin bellies just one hundred feet above our heads, the roar taking our breath away. Our world was a postcard of moonlit water and swaying palms, the glamour of it intoxicating. We were under the influence of the Florida moon and the God who had made it shine.

My time spent at the Bible college was the best time of my life. The background music was laughter that derived from fun and joy. The fun came from friends, common bonds, and good times. The joy came from God. I had centered my life and immersed myself in his presence. The spiritual disciplines of early morning prayer and Bible reading encouraged me to rely on God for guidance and wisdom. I could feel myself getting stronger mentally, emotionally, and spiritually. This strength was not something I had mustered up; it was a gift from God. I had reached up, and the God of the universe had bent down.

But each May, I was awakened from this tropical dream to spend the summer in Pennsylvania working as a bank teller. The bank's president, who attended our church, had recommended me for the job. I liked the job and seemed to have a knack for the business world, which allowed me to make money and catch up with people I had left behind. Pennsylvania didn't have a moonlit ocean, but it did have the auburn-haired girl.

The first few summers, I resumed my relationship with the auburn-haired girl. But each time I left for school again, the distance took an increasingly bigger toll. Then one day our relationship was gone, dissolved by too many hours spent apart in different worlds. There was no formal breakup—only a good-bye with no subsequent hello. I was relieved. No longer doing something I felt I shouldn't, my guilt was finally gone. I could now be stamped "Approved" and return to school freed of the deepest secret I had ever held.

I had kept almost everybody at school in the dark about my sexual past except my best friend, Trudy. Trudy had been part of our group since our freshman year, and we had become inseparable. Her petite frame and quirky style made her the yin to my yang; she was an original, out-of-the-box thinker. Instinctively, I knew I could trust her with my secret. She didn't freak out, but she did make it clear that she didn't approve— and at times she refused to even acknowledge that my inappropriate relationship existed. When I brought it up, she would appear shocked, as if this were the first time I had delivered the news. When the relationship with the auburn-haired girl came to an end, I never told Trudy it was over, and she never asked. It was a subject that had become unmentionable. Other than that we were each other's greatest support.

By my junior year, I was deeply committed to the college and its staff. I had been reelected student council secretary for an unprecedented third term. During the school years I had always worked outside of the college as a maid or a cashier, but in my junior year I began to work part-time within the college, first in the admissions office and later also as a caregiver to the president's elderly mother.

As I went from freshman, to sophomore, to junior year, my pastor-wife wedding clock ticked on unnoticed in the busyness of my life. I could go for weeks without a thought about my pending dilemma until someone would mention the impending graduation. Then an alarm would go off, causing concern about what I would need to do to find someone soon. I had seen other girls almost magically decide it was time to find a man and it would happen, but I didn't know how they did it. I wondered why God was not helping me with this part of the plan for my life. But I realized I needed to keep my eyes open to new possibilities.

I was usually open to new experiences, but when my friends suggested a Saturday evening bluegrass concert in the auditorium, at first I wasn't sure if it was for me. Being from the North, I thought bluegrass was like bad country music; with the television show *Hee Haw* having been my only exposure to it, all I could remember was the twang of nasal-toned songs. Eventually, though, I agreed to the concert, and it was great fun. We hooted, hollered, laughed, and enjoyed every minute of the band's enormous musical talent. These young men were all music majors planning to become music ministers in churches across America, leading choirs and coordinating other musical events. While each day at chapel services we had heard many talented student musicians, this fantastic ensemble of grit and grace was new to me. Out of the blue, bluegrass had touched me.

Within a week I began dating the band's guitar player, knowing I needed to put myself in the playing field if I was ever going to find my pastor mate. Whatever was holding me back needed to be eliminated, so I spent a lot of time with the guitar player; I hung on his arm; I was his girl. But as much as I tried to open my heart to him, he was not my man. After two months, the brakes in my heart went on. I realized the deep attachment that needed to be there for me to love or marry a man was absent. On the outside, it looked like we were in love; but on the inside, this match wasn't for me. My mind conjured up reasons for the relationship's demise, wondering how could I, a northern women's libber-type, spend the rest of my life with a guitar player from the Deep South and picturing days spent picking cotton and wrestling alligators. Ultimately, the bluegrass guitar player became another victim of a quick good-bye.

I told myself I just hadn't found the right man. But deep inside I was beginning to come to terms with my reality—that perhaps no guy would ever do and, if not, my future in church service would be in jeopardy. Then I considered the option that I might need to change my idea of love. Maybe it was enough to marry a great guy with a good future. Maybe the sparks weren't necessary. When I allowed myself to think this way, I could feel a pit opening in my stomach, an emotional void. I was sure such a union would be a self-inflicted life sentence of dull days and endless nights. Many days I ignored the conflict, still believing that with God's help my prince would come. Yet despite all my hopes of finding true love with a man, I knew I would not settle for mediocre. I could not just admire a man; I needed to be passionately in love. Although I was only fleetingly willing to acknowledge it, a more serious and brutal inner battle about my sexuality had begun.

CHAPTER 9

Falling in Love,
Falling from Grace

In the spring of 1979, my junior year in college, my world as I had known it was forever changed when I unexpectedly fell in love with a woman then suffered devastating consequences at the hands of school officials. I had been working in the college admissions office for a year but decided I was ready for something new, so I took a job in the college snack shop, swapping paperwork for food prep. This new job didn't feel like work; the steady flow of new faces was a perfect fit for my extroverted personality.

I had been on the job less than a week when somewhere between the yogurt case and the meat slicer I caught a glimpse of the large smiling blue eyes of a woman. Those eyes were part of an adorable little face that didn't just smile but beamed. In total, the woman, whose name was Lisa, was a tiny ball of fire wrapped in a package of sweetness and tied with a ribbon named delight. As her new trainee, I was to spend weeks working side by side with her, preparing food, but underneath the daily tasks an unmistakable attraction was building. With this attraction came questions: Is she or isn't she? What are her thoughts behind the long-lashed glances? Did I misconstrue sweeps of her hand for chances to touch my skin? Were the touches simply because of our close quarters or did they mean something more? My questioning eyes were longing for answers that I was not sure I wanted to know, anxious, perhaps, that playing with a tiny ball of fire had the potential to catalyze a five-alarm blaze.

As our friendship grew, we started to work together in student ministries. One day Lisa and I spent several hours with a group of eight students at a mall. It was a typical evangelistic event in which the college students talked to people who wanted to hear about Jesus. The day had gone well; many people had been receptive. During the ride home, we shared our thoughts with one another and prayed that our messages had had a positive effect on the lives of those who had heard the good news. Our elation was the fuel that made the tiny ball of fire burst into the blaze I had feared.

In the van, we knew the attraction had reached its pinnacle. An unspoken understanding then prompted us to take the elevator to her room. Washed in the white hot sun of the late Florida afternoon, we did not even dare to glance at each other as our internal questioning was about to become reality. My heart thumped in my ears. A knot of wrong versus right was lodged in my throat. I sat on the bed, nervous at the thought of her roommate finding us alone, sure the guilt of my thoughts was shouting loud enough to give away my intention. One minute, I secretly wished for her roommate to appear; the next I hoped her roommate would stay away for hours.

Lisa sat on the bed next to me, our thighs touching and our pent-up desires of the past months driving us forward. She turned her head and softly kissed my cheek. I responded immediately with lips acting on months of desire. I had the answers to my questions. We were both willing, and we were both definitely gay.

I have been told that the average person cannot take into account the full consequences of their actions until their late twenties. I could have been the poster child for that idea. Lust and longing for love were all that had significance in my actions with Lisa—caution was not part of the mix. Maybe my prominence at the school had made me overconfident, and I thought such an affair could not take me down. Maybe the devil saw this as a way to wreck my chances for ministry. I knew the rules and that I was breaking them. I also knew the consequences could be life altering.

I was living in the most uncompromising of situations. I was in the Christian South at a time when gays remained in the closet. To most people in mainstream America, the homosexual lifestyle was not welcome. The only people who were gay and accepted were urban eccentrics and artists, as well as an occasional edgy hair stylist. All others needed to deny their homosexual tendencies and remain in the closet buried in shame.

This is how most of America viewed homosexuality, and it was exaggerated in the conservative state of Florida. Around this time, the famous beauty-queen-turned-orange-juice-promoter Anita Bryant was campaigning for something completely different from the morning juice choice. The slogan "Breakfast without orange juice is like a day without sunshine" was replaced by the chant "Save Our Children." Her nationally publicized campaign against gays was being fought in the county directly to our south. Located within twenty miles of our college, the Save Our Children coalition was established to fight a proposed amendment to the local law advocating against discrimination based on sexual orientation. Bryant truly believed that the Bible spoke against homosexuality, which was nothing new. But an aspect of her platform that evoked fear was her claim that homosexuals had an aggressive agenda, that since homosexuals are not able to have their own biological children they would do their best to recruit other people's children to the homosexual lifestyle. The whole South, with help from Gerry Falwell, stood behind her in the fight against Florida's newly emerging gay population. Ultimately, the Save Our Children campaign was successful in squelching the amendment, leaving discrimination against sexual orientation legal.

Our college heralded Bryant's efforts as a wonderful victory, championing her cause from the pulpit during daily services and decorating the student union with newspaper clippings proclaiming: "Morality Has Triumphed Over the Evils of Homosexuality." As crowds gathered around the newsprint, my heart skipped a beat. Being gay in a community that was intolerant of gays meant I was an outcast, ostracized by my peers while living in their midst. My actions were invisible to them, yet I knew that if they were known a verbal lynching would be inevitable. I did not want anyone to even think of my name in the same sentence with Anita Bryant's.

Yet I had no thought of ending the relationship with Lisa—or slowing down. I was high on life but could tell no one about the beautiful remedy for my loneliness. I knew the school's policy, but I also knew that my feelings for Lisa were strong and real, and risky. I was guiltless about my love; I only feared the consequences it could bring.

I will never know exactly where lust stopped and love started with Lisa. My lust compelled me to use my authority and my master key to spend nights in unoccupied dorm rooms alone with Lisa. Lust led me to lie to my friends. Lust made me lose my mind. Lust is not constructive. Lust has one pathway, called Heartache, which often dead-ends in destruction. I am deeply ashamed about my sin driven by this untamed monster.

But lust was not the only element in our bond; we were also in love. I loved everything about Lisa. It was young love, foolish love. While it crossed my mind that I might be ruining my career, I also knew that although our love was on a mission to crash and burn I could seemingly do nothing to stop it—nor did I want to. I swore I could feel sparks as I touched Lisa's warm skin, and experienced emotions stronger than I had previously thought possible. I had found what my heart had been missing. Men had never managed to light such a flame. I wanted my love to be accepted, but I knew that this would never happen. We spoke of a future ministry together, closeted to the world yet blissfully happy in each other's arms, but the conversation would always end with sadness, knowing that such a future could never be.

I was now both one of the in-crowd and one of the despised. I believed God loved me but not my sin, and I accepted this theology in theory, though I could not bring myself to call the love I had for Lisa a sin. I was living a lie, and my days were wonderful yet miserable. I believed God was not happy, perhaps angry. What I didn't know was how much I should have feared humankind. Amidst the climate of hatred for homosexuals all around me, somehow I didn't think it applied to me. I only knew that I loved God and I loved Lisa. For some reason, I could not see the edge of the precipice.

As Lisa and I became closer, my relationship with my roommate and best friend, Trudy, began to slip away. Even though we did not speak about the situation, she was the only one who could have guessed the source of my torture since she had to have known what kept me away from our dorm room most nights. Her worried looks told me she knew I was in trouble, and her silences revealed the conflict she felt between keeping me out of trouble and believing that I was not obeying God.

I was glad when May came and I could be away from her questioning gaze. I left for home emotionally conflicted between what I had been taught was wrong by the people I admired most and what I was experiencing to be true. I spent the summer two thousand miles from Lisa, during which time the flames died to embers but the heat remained.

Despite my inner conflicts, my desire for ministry remained. Without a husband, I figured, I could perhaps still have a bright future if I refocused my employment objectives. In larger churches, women were starting to be hired as Christian education directors, a position that involved selecting curricula and staff, and maintaining Sunday School activities. I knew I would never make much money but would be content to serve God and have him meet my needs. God was my ultimate goal and my means. I had used that same sentiment in my reelection speech for senior class secretary, quoting the Apostle Paul from Philippians 1:21:

"For me to live is Christ and to die is gain." I meant those words from the very core of my being.

I began my senior year of college with the promise of graduation and hopes of a future career. A role in Christian education was my new goal, and I had to make sure nothing would stand in my way. Lisa and I had started the semester with fresh determination to control our passion by maintaining our distance. We worked opposite schedules. We took different classes. We tried to avoid crossing paths. But the plan didn't work. The school building that once seemed so grand was now too small, and the lure was too great.

People raised with my theological background may believe that this part of my story was a victory for Satan. They may say that God had great plans to use me but those plans were thwarted by my misjudgment and sin. These same thoughts would lead them to a comparison with the story of King David, who was driven to murder, and the near demise of his throne over a beautiful woman he saw bathing on a rooftop. Such people would conclude: these women were caught up in sinful lust since a relationship between two women could not possibly be based on love. They would pronounce one of two judgments—either the women were not daughters of God in the first place or they were deeply in need of repentance. Then the gavel would drop and the sinners would be pronounced guilty. But while I was aware of such judgments and the sentence that would be inflicted, this information did not resonate with my innermost beliefs.

Eventually, Trudy became so concerned about her suspicions that she confided in a professor, action she told me she took because of her love for me. I had no reason to doubt the sincerity of her motive, but I don't believe she had calculated the cost to me. Within two hours, the professor had gone to the vice president. Within three hours, judgment was delivered at lightning speed.

In the midst of a class, I was tapped on the shoulder from behind by the dean of women, whose face bore an expression of dismay and fear. I followed her out, hoping that my gut instinct to flee was coming from my guilt and not the truth behind her summons. The hallway's narrow, yellow-cream walls seemed to engulf me in dread, its bright fluorescent lights bouncing in my eyes from the low ceilings overhead. This was the hallway where the administrative offices were located, where I had once said to myself, "I belong." I moved stiffly, almost paralyzed with fear. I had walked this hall as an insider, a helper, a servant and fellow lover of Christ, but this time I walked surrounded by the aura of terror and the shame of disgrace.

The vice president ushered me into his windowless office and motioned toward a guest chair that faced his massive desk. My knees crumbled involuntarily to a seating position. The dean of women was seated along the wall behind me and to the left. In my altered state, although her head was cocked to the side in concern, it appeared to be screwed on at an unnatural right angle. Her bottle-blonde hair hung from the crooked tilt in glimmering sheets, partly covering her elongated face. The dean of women, then in her late thirties and possibly the most powerful woman on campus, was someone I had known for at least ten years and, up until this moment, had called Linda. She had been my youth pastor's wife who helped me find my calling and inspired me to opt for a lifetime of Christian work. They had arrived at this college a year before me as husband and wife. He had been offered a professorship, while she had been given a role in administration. She was to be the witness. It is not unusual in the Christian community to call a witness when someone is telling another person about their wrongdoings, but this was certainly not going to be the average encourage-one-another speech.

The vice president, handsome and built like a football player, settled in behind his desk. His dark, slick shiny hair, perfectly ironed white shirts, and the forever tan of a Floridian usually oozed charm and confidence. But today he was nervous, angry, and grave. I turned to Linda, but the woman who sat to my left in the shadows was no longer the Linda I had known. What remained was the stony dean of women, set on carrying out the letter of the law. There was no remembrance of the love I had lavished on the college community or the service I had given to the school. There would be no safety net.

The vice president showed no emotion as he pulled a tape recorder out of his desk drawer and asked if I would mind if our discussion was taped. Somewhere between numb and terrified, I agreed. I confessed that I had indeed been in an inappropriate sexual relationship with Lisa. Only a few other words were spoken; that was all the record they needed. No counseling was offered, no prayer for guidance said. My years of service were forgotten. My love for God was ignored. I did not beg for mercy. I knew the rules, and I did not blame the college officials. Finally, the vice president told me in a businesslike tone that I had twenty-four hours to leave the premises. My expulsion was swift and brutal. They did not ask if I had somewhere to go. In a matter of minutes, I had transformed from golden child to disgraced leper. God had shown grace in the salvation of my soul, but there was apparently no grace available for the current situation. This man and woman whom I had adored could not find a caring word to offer. I knew if I could have died right there it would have solved many problems. I didn't know what to tell people or where to go. In one taped confession my life of joy and my hopes for the future had been erased.

With twenty-four hours to leave the premises, I had to make a plan quickly. Although still in shock, I found the strength to cross the lower-level lobby to the phone booth. With my hands shaking, my ears ringing, my heart thumping in my ears, I called my mother and finally said the words I had hoped I would never have to utter: "Mom, I got kicked out of school because I am gay." I had to say those words to someone whose mantra was "What will the neighbors think?" Upon finding out that her daughter was leaving college in her senior year, people would probably think I had gotten pregnant or had had an affair with a married student, or I had changed my mind about loving God. My words were said to a mother who believed that homosexuality was a sin. I wondered if she would accept me back into her home and still love me, or if I would be out on the street, losing my family the same day I lost my hopes for a future in the ministry. I had taken the gamble; besides, I had nowhere else to turn. I knew my mother had wondered about my sexual identity before since I had had many sleepovers with the auburn-haired girl and my mother had often referenced our odd relationship. But I knew she had not wanted to face that as a reality.

After a silence, she replied, simply, "Oh, Susie." Her voice did not express anger or disbelief. Instead, it reflected a crushing realization of the truth, confirmation of her fear. But what amazed me was the maturity of her reaction. She had responded with a mother's love that looked beyond her own cares. A parent who called homosexuality a sin, a parent who had been so proud of a daughter headed toward full-time ministry became the parent of a daughter with no future in the church but disgrace. Now our dreams were gone.

In less than twenty-four hours, I picked her up at the Fort Lauderdale airport. Back at school, we packed my room in a stupor. The disgrace lay heavy; my head was numb. I did not reveal the details to those I chose to tell of my departure. My mother and I headed north on I-95 back to Pennsylvania. We steered, accelerated, and applied the brakes, but our spirits within had been silenced. The trip was as dismal as if someone had died, which in a way was true: all my hopes for graduation and a life of service to God in the ministry had died. I tried not to look out the car windows, as each mile traveled seemed to confirm that my world was slipping farther and farther away.

Back home I sank into a depression as I attempted to come to grips with the truth. My actions had been my fault. I had known the rules, and I had not followed them. I did not eat; I did not speak. My mother did not judge with words or ask any questions, perhaps afraid of the answers. Three and a half years earlier, I had left her to fight her own fears in God's hands to find who she was on her own. Without me, she had indeed found strength. She now sat by my side for hours coaxing me from my catatonic state and urging me to eat. Our roles were now reversed: the parent was once again the parent. She had risen to the occasion in my hour of need.

My future in the Christian ministry now seemed hopeless. The weeks crawled by as I mourned. Cocooned within familiar walls, I assigned myself the daily task of breathing through the shame. In the process, my relationship with Lisa quickly became part of a past I wanted to forget. Now I grieved alone for the beautiful life I had lost. My mother knew why I had been expelled, but she was not able—and I was not willing—to discuss the details of my relationship with the woman I had left behind. I wondered what had made me think that I could get away with my actions and not incur the school's wrath. Both shame and grief became a powerful crashing wave drowning me in loss, and I seemed to have no way to get off the emotional treadmill that tormented me.

CHAPTER 10

Collecting the Pieces of My Existence

WHILE I WAS AT HOME RECOVERING from having been dismissed and disgraced by the Bible college, my mother attempted to minimize the fallout by keeping our closest relatives in the dark regarding my dismissal. I did not fight her plan. Having come out to my mother under duress, I was glad to avoid giving more explanations. In many families, truths are not told unless asked for. Some people don't ask because they believe certain matters are not their business; others are afraid of the answers they might receive; still others do not want to know since knowing requires offering comfort or responding in some other way. For these reasons and more, my mother did not want our relatives to know of either my disgrace or the guilt she bore.

The only person my mother told was my sister, probably needing someone with whom to share her grief. Neither of them told me they had spoken about my circumstances, but the atmosphere changed in an obvious way when the three of us were together. Actually, I was glad my sister had been informed since it meant there was one more person who knew the truth about my circumstances and still cared about me.

After a few weeks, though, I needed words of comfort, so I phoned my youth pastor at church. He was willing to meet, but before we met he made sure I realized that he already knew the reason I was home. The Bible college had called my church to make our pastoral staff aware of my tendency toward relationships with girls. This did not strike me as a violation of privacy but only one more thing I deserved for having fallen from grace. But I did wonder why the pastor had not called to minister to me in my state of obvious need. No matter what his reason for not coming to my aid, I was glad the youth pastor was willing to talk, so I headed over to his office. When we met, he maintained his cool demeanor, but I perceived that counseling a lesbian was a new and flustering experience for him. The man who always seemed to have plenty to say was now searching for words. Finally, he blushed and said, "You just haven't been with the right man yet. If you knew how it could be, I am certain it would fix you right up." Because these were ideas I had told myself during my earlier struggle to date boys, my face surely reflected the fact that I felt he was completely clueless. Maybe it was my femininity that threw him. Maybe he thought that what I experienced had been only a fling, or perhaps he had no understanding of the feelings involved in homosexual relationships. Realizing his ignorance and feeling a new sense of loneliness, I headed home conscious that one more person of the cloth could not help me. These were people I revered, and I was shocked at how ill-equipped they were to offer comfort. I wondered if there was anyone I could turn to.

As weeks passed, the deep clouds of depression and disgrace that surrounded me thinned to a haze. I did not see hatred or evil in those who had treated me poorly. I saw only my own weakness, my sin as the source of my troubles. But I knew I could not remain in the depths of depression forever, that even with all my self-loathing I had to go on. My mother encouraged me to call the bank to see if I could return to work there. They asked me no questions and were thrilled to have me back. I welcomed this news, rejoicing that God was reaching down to love me in my darkest hour. The job got me out of the house and functioning in the world again.

The people at church also didn't ask me why I had dropped out of school. Yet a lot of heads turned. But before they could speculate for very long, I applied at the local Bible college for the spring semester, making them think I must have come home to finish my education there. The local Bible college was accredited, so I would be getting a real degree. My mother was thrilled, perceiving this as a way to save her daughter from disgrace. I had never given up the desire to finish my education and do full-time Christian work. My love for God had not diminished; I still believed I had been called into the ministry. With a new plan for the future, I felt I had to kick my gay behavior for good and even contemplated resuming my search for Mr. Right.

But by now I had turned a corner. I had loved the auburn-haired girl. I had loved Lisa so much that I had been willing to risk my future for her. I knew I was gay. I knew I had not found a man yet who could fulfill my emotions and desires as these two women had done so easily. I had to acknowledge that there was nothing I could do to make myself romantically love the opposite sex; I had tried and failed miserably. I had always relied on God to find me the right man. But now my prayers shifted focus, acknowledging that this was not something I could fix and asking God to change my heart. I could not muster feelings for a man or change my behavior on my own, and I needed to put my future into the hands of a loving God. I was fully aware that I was at the mercy of the hearts and minds of the new people in charge of my future. The local college did not have to accept me; my circumstances could have stopped the enrollment process. But I was sure God would be the ultimate judge of my fate. All I wanted was to get in, to get on with my studies and my calling.

On a sunny cold day in early January 1980, I was summoned to the new school's admissions office. The call, coming from a school administrator, had evoked self-protected fear within me. Wandering into the college building, with its sterile green 1950s concrete block walls, felt all wrong. The grandeur of the Florida hotel, the special place I had called home, had been replaced by a facility that was cold and uninviting. The enormity of what I had lost reemerged, pressing down on my head and shoulders; my heart submerged deeper in my chest. Weak-kneed, I pressed on through the sterile halls and down the rubber-tipped linoleum steps to the subterranean admissions office one story below the earth. I stepped inside and sat down, taking in the color of the light and shadows from the basement window above.

The person who sat across the desk had no face in my memory, no sex, and no particular personality. The talking head began by telling me there had been a lengthy conversation with the Bible college in Florida, as courses had needed to be compared to determine which ones would count as credits and which ones I would still need. There had been polite words about my work on the student council and about my academic achievements. My homosexual behavior had been discussed at length. The matter had then been taken before the board, words that caused a jolt of panic in my already pounding chest. I could only imagine what kind of discussion my scandalous actions must have started. I sat in dread as I readied myself for rejection. But by the time my mind had registered what had been said, the talking head was speaking about start dates and Christmas break. My inner state eventually caught up with the notion that I had been accepted—without scolding words or warnings about future indiscretions—allowing me to finish my journey.

However, I soon learned that the acceptance came with some strings attached. One stipulation involved having to extend my studies. Although I had been twelve credits short of graduating when I had left Florida, since all my credits had not been accepted I now had to earn fifty-four more to complete my degree. I had had one semester to go when I left, and now it would take an additional year and a half, or possibly two. Yet the news did not obstruct my goal or dampen my determination. My calling was still strong, and I needed to graduate.

The second stipulation was that I undergo psychological testing.

Consequently, I spent an afternoon answering questions and filling in dots with a No. 2 pencil. I tested normal. In fact, I appeared quite well adjusted. I am not sure what they made of my normalcy, but despite the outcome I was required to attend weekly meetings with the school's approved psychologist.

I arrived at his office for my first visit at 6:00 pm one evening in February. The professional building was a squat brown-on-brown structure in a row of boring architecture. The empty parking lot was lifeless in the after hours, with only the light standards alive, throwing their round shapes onto the pavement below. I opened the door; he was the only one there. The office was dark, except for a lamp that gave just enough of a glow to supposedly make me feel at home. The psychologist greeted me with a serious doctor voice appropriate to the task at hand. I was amazed that I wasn't nervous, embarrassed, or frightened. *Perhaps I'm getting used to the idea of exposing my shame*, I thought to myself. More likely, I was ready for help to find my way to freedom. As we were seated facing one another, I took in his appearance. I estimated he was in his late fifties, tall but not particularly handsome; the most pronounced feature was his beard, which was an odd shade of brown-gray and flawlessly groomed. Three inches of straight hair outlined the periphery of his face. For all intents, he should have looked like a porcupine, but instead his beard seemed to defy gravity by curving in a perfect puff around his jaw and chin, displaying a masterpiece of engineering. The name Mr. Anti-Gravity Beard leapt to my mind as suitable. I readied myself for words of healing.

Moments passed as he tried to find his first words. His interview began with the words "They tell me you think you are a homosexual. What makes you think that?" My first thought was, *Are you kidding me?* But I managed to mumble something about being attracted to women. His next question was, "Well, what did you do with your (uncomfortable pause) your . . . this other girl?" My second thought was, *Are you kidding me? After all I have been through, these are the words you have to offer?* The next questions were just as brilliant: "Did you kiss her? Did your physical relationship go further?" Out of respect and wanting to fulfill my obligation, I provided him with enough information about our physical relationship to give him a picture of a lesbian sex life without the graphic details. In between my answers, I tried to keep my mouth from hanging open in disbelief. It was clear he was at a total loss for treating my condition. After taking a deep breath, he admitted that I was a feminine, beautiful young woman and that he needed to make sure I understood what a lesbian was. My frustration level was reaching its peak. There were a million sarcastic answers that banged back and forth in my head. I wanted to say, *No, I just got kicked out of college, but I am not really sure what a lesbian is. Can you fill me in?* But I did not think he was being lewd, so I kept quiet.

My hope of finishing Bible college made me return. For three months, I made weekly visits to Mr. Anti-Gravity Beard before he dismissed me from his care. I don't remember one productive thing from our encounters and even caught him nodding off during one of my answers. But once the sessions were over, I had fulfilled my obligation to the new school. Apparently I wasn't crazy. I did not receive any feedback from the school, and I never saw a written report from the psychologist. I still wanted to be "set free," but I knew this man had not been the one to even remotely begin the process. I concluded I wanted to go to school and never be in this situation again.

The new school was different in many ways. Florida had been my nirvana. Its missionary zeal and soul-searching academics had meshed perfectly with my spirit. In this new school, the higher academic standards left little time for the Spirit to work. Appearance was paramount. Dancing, drinking, and movies were prohibited, but not because of any word from God. The Spirit was given no freedom for deciding what you should and shouldn't do; the school decided for you. Academics and the mind took precedence over the heart and soul. When we learned, we learned volumes fast, but there was seldom time to apply any new knowledge to actions and activities where heart and Spirit played a role (Galatians 5:25). This type of Christianity was not for me, but I remained focused on why I was there—to study and graduate so I could go into the ministry.

In addition, I commuted to the school, limiting my interactions with fellow students, which to me felt like a form of social exile. I had been involved in everything in Florida, but here I was a ghostlike observer, watching student life pass me by. There was no laughter, no leadership, not only at the new school but personally; my former self had been shattered. Feeling alone and out of place, at this point I wasn't even sure who I was. I came to the conclusion that no one in this new and very different world really cared about what I had to offer. The pieces of my existence were scattered, and I was alone with God to collect what was left of them and try to move forward. Where God would lead me, I did not know. He would have to open the doors to my future.

CHAPTER 11

Dating an Alien

AFTER MONTHS OF GRIEVING, I emerged into the light, and soon the huge hole in my soul was being filled by the many activities of the church youth group. I do not know what was said behind closed doors, but the church staff decided to allow me to serve. The pastor who had counseled me about "being with the right man" was now in charge of the youth. Unexpectedly, I was back at the pivotal point of my youth, when I had been called to full-time ministry, only this time I was a leader.

After a three-year absence, I was happy to see that the youth group was still going strong. Members were bringing other kids from their high schools in record numbers, so there were new faces at each meeting. At one gathering, a new student, Doug, caught my eye. Tall and lean with dark hair and freckles, he seemed to be the central figure of a group of five male students, all clearly hanging on his words. He was young, only in eleventh grade, but the esteem others showed him indicated to me that he was something special. I was told he was a star long-distance runner. I was attracted to him, and he was a male; maybe it wasn't too late for me to try again. So even though it was a totally new concept for me to ask a guy out, I mustered up my best women's libber courage and asked Doug out on a date. We went to an art museum. It felt more like being with a buddy than a boyfriend, but I was doing my best to conform. I wanted to feel normal; I was hoping to be normal.

So began my two-and-a-half-year relationship with an alien being. At twenty-one, I had yet to develop any deep friendships with men. I had become so at home with women that I considered any relationship with the opposite sex an extraterrestrial experience. I could not understand what women saw in these aliens. I did not see gender in terms of the cosmos, like the cutesy Mars and Venus differences proposed in a popular book. To me, the starship *Enterprise* could not reach that farthest galaxy where man must have originated. I knew they ate and slept. I knew they worked and joked. But I was not quite sure what was going on inside them. I was under the impression that men's emotional makeup was underdeveloped and somehow originated in an area between their stomachs and groins. But I needed to delve into the psyche of such an alien to see if, somehow, I could be the lesbian pioneer who would cross light years of unchartered space to arrive at the far-off destination of heterosexuality.

Although my relationship with the alien was a bit unconventional, the pastoral staff cheered us on, no doubt thrilled at the prospect that the problem woman might have found a way out of her sinful behavior. I knew they were watching me and was almost sure I could be back in the graces of the church's leadership if I had found the right man. Aware of the obstacles to be overcome and yet hopeful that my past troubles would be erased, I gladly submitted to going through the motions of a woman in a heterosexual relationship.

I tried to ignore the differences in age and experience between us. I had experienced the death of a parent and struggle with my sexual orientation. Being younger, he had a sweet innocence but limited experience in the world. Initially, the physical relationship was there; the time spent was there; and excitement of new romance was there. But once again the relationship lacked honest communication, emotional intensity, and intimacy. The lack of communication was largely my fault. I had made a conscious decision that I was not going to tell him my story, for reasons that seemed perfectly logical. My homosexual exploits were part of my past, I was doing my best to believe that feelings for women would not be part of my future, and I was sure he was not mature enough to absorb the truth without rejecting me. As for the lack of emotional connection and intimacy reminiscent of my past relationships with men, I tried my best to ignore its glaring absence. So we made our way through everyday life keeping our conversations in a safe zone.

But as our relationship stagnated, I realized I had not come to terms with my inability to relate emotionally to this wonderful young man. Fear and the deep feeling that anyone I might turn to would not be able to help, stopped me from confiding in anyone about this problem. I was sure that if I opened up about my inability to feel deeply for Doug, whomever I told would know that I was gay.

As the months went on, the alien's kindness and leadership abilities made me proud to be his girlfriend, and I hoped I could fall in love with him. But in quiet moments doubts would rise to the surface like the Ghosts of Christmas Past. When considering my boyfriends of the past, I could see I was following an undeniable pattern despite my hope that God was going to change me. There was no way I could deny the disconnection I felt with Doug. I just couldn't get my heart to believe what my mind knew was best. I thought that if this is how it was supposed to be between men and women, I couldn't settle for such an expressionless void. I just couldn't seem to bridge the interplanetary gap. He was special; and I could only hang on and hope that if God considered being gay a sin, he would change me. I continued to pray and leave my heart in God's hands.

At the time I was caught up in my love affair with an alien, life was busier than ever. With more than a full load of college credits each semester, I still managed to get at least a 3.0 grade point average. Added to that load was my part-time work at the bank and my volunteer work at church. It was a schedule that could lead to madness and would soon have dire consequences. One night I woke out of a dead sleep with an intense pain in my stomach, as if I had digested shards of glass. I went downstairs to my mother's room and told her I needed to go to the hospital. She still partially blamed herself for not insisting that my father go to the hospital the night he had been so ill, so off we went to the emergency room. After being observed, I was given medicine to calm the spasms and sent home to rest, with no conclusive diagnosis.

But my studies and my job gave me no time to rest, and I was soon back in the same frenzied lifestyle. The pain soon became a pattern. It would reappear every few weeks, gradually intensifying from grinding to nausea to severe vomiting and ultimately a trip to the hospital for a series of tests. Sometimes they would keep me overnight for observation, while other times they would sedate me and send me home; in either case, by the next day I would be tired but fine. After the fourth or fifth trip, the head physician proclaimed that he was not letting me go home until they finally discovered what was wrong with me, but after another full battery of tests no cause was found.

Eventually, my mother heard from one of her girlfriends that a family doctor who had recently started a practice in town had been the only one able to diagnose her friend's illness. We promptly made an appointment with him. He was a bit odd-looking; with fuzzy hair and perfectly square protruding front teeth, he had the appearance of an oversized friendly bunny, but he got right to the point. He said, "Tell me about your life." When I described my hectic schedule, he waved his hand to stop me, prescribed Valium, and declared, "Come back to me next week and tell me what activities you have eliminated from your life." It had been obvious to him that the pain was caused by stress. I began to wonder if my stomach pain was actually my body's way of rebelling because I was betraying its natural psychological and physical inclinations by being involved with a man. Yet, like everything else that focused on my homosexuality, I quickly dismissed the thought.

With the pain managed by a moderate amount of Valium, I did not sever ties with the alien being because of physical problems, but there were now other difficulties with the relationship. Doug's parents did not like their prized son, from whom they expected great things, dating a woman five years older. They wanted him to play the field and experience life. And they certainly didn't want him to marry someone so involved with the Baptist church. They attended a Methodist church on Sundays and felt the Baptists were far too religious and strict for their lifestyle. The feeling was mutual. The Baptists called the Methodists "Sunday seekers," for whom God made a difference in their lives only between 11:00 am and 12:00 pm on Sundays. The Baptists concluded that the Methodist church was a tidy place with a social club feel.

My boyfriend's parents fit the bill. They were beautiful people mingling with others of like kind. While far from measuring up to their social status, on some days I began to think seriously of marriage; after all, I had a great man who was going to be somebody after getting through a few more years of college. I told myself his parents would come around and I would do my best to be a great daughter-in-law. But on other days I questioned whether the feelings I had for him were enough for entering into a lifetime commitment.

CHAPTER 12

Unexpected Meeting with a Mermaid

IN THE SUMMER OF 1981, with one year left of college and still no definite plan for my future, I remained hopeful that my dream of full-time Christian work would come true. I would start searching for a job at the end of the next semester. But for now it was time to forget the future and enjoy the warmth of the sun and the pleasures of summer.

One warm, sunny Saturday afternoon with a perfect blue sky, the youth group had a pool party. I stood next to the water, taking great delight in watching everyone horse around with their friends. The pool water was its customary violent mass of waves from the competitive game of keep-away they were playing. The game was at full tilt when, out of a struggle between opponents, a new face emerged from under the water. The oval face, with its dark complexion and large brown eyes, held an expression of playfulness, while its long, thick lashes glistening with droplets of water, deep dimples set below high cheekbones, and a wide, white smile evoked the freshness of youth. The water cascaded down the woman's short dark hair and onto her broad, muscled shoulders. Her shining face and vigorous body were lit from within with the glow of strength, causing the backdrop of the pool to suddenly fade into a wash of gray. The woman's beaming face and strong body had captured my attention as if she were the only thing still existing on the earth. It was like seeing a mysterious mermaid.

Not yet realizing the magnitude of this encounter, I shook it off and walked back to my life with the alien. But I kept wondering who this woman was and why I would allow such thoughts to enter my mind after the disgrace and pain I had recently experienced. I knew the Christians at church were my people, my brothers and sisters. They had not inflicted the pain; rather, I had not played by the rules on their court, causing self-inflicted wounds. They had taken me in limping and bloody and had nursed me back to a semblance of myself. How could I now turn my back on them and cause more pain by acting on impulses they called sin?

I tried my best to talk some sense into myself. With the recent trouble and heartache still raw within me, I was fully aware that acting in keeping with my true sexual orientation would jeopardize my future and hurt others, who would not approve. Yet there was something about the mystery woman I could not ignore.

I didn't meet her until a month or so later, but I did ask about her. I discovered that her name was Beth and she was one of the younger children in a large, prominent family at our twelve-hundred-member church where her grandfather was a pastor. Had I been sane, I would have run in the other direction. But I didn't; as it turned out, I might as well have allowed myself to have feelings for Billy Graham's daughter or run naked down the church aisle and get it over with or emblazon a large L on my chest and speak at the women's retreat. Instead, I simply asked myself how I had missed noticing her before now. I was told she hadn't been coming to youth group because she was her high school's star basketball and softball athlete, activities that had taken up much of her time. Now that school was out till the fall, I hoped I would be seeing more of her. The combination of my attraction to her and my decision to throw caution to the wind sent me hurtling toward more destruction.

Subsequently, she did start to attend the Thursday evening youth group. Like the rest of her family, she was musical. Her dad played the trumpet, her mom played the organ, her sister played the piano, her brother was a music major, and Beth played the guitar. They all sang, too. The von Trapps had nothing on this family. The star of the show was Beth, whose voice had the depth of Karen Carpenter's and the folk style of Norah Jones. It was the auditory equivalent of having layers of satin drape across your naked skin. If you closed your eyes while listening, you would be transported to another world. Beth's older sisters had previously helped with the singing at the youth group, and now Beth became fully involved as well. I liked to sing, and even though I sounded like a squealing tire by comparison, we often led youth group singing together and soon became good friends. Our times together were full of laughter and a common purpose; then at the end of our practice the alien would be there, patiently waiting to take me home—without demands, only doing what boyfriends do. Leaving with the alien was like tumbling from an elevated sphere of song to the flat, silent world below.

During the year or so I spent getting to know Beth, I learned to think of love as having the qualities of fine art. I began to realize that the time I spent with Doug was colored in shades of beige. Our relationship was like a Monet painting: viewed too closely, it was blurry and muted; the focus was off; the picture was not whole. In contrast, the time I spent with Beth was a classic Cassatt painting, with bright yellows, blues, and oranges reflecting a fevered pitch of excitement about life. I knew where I wanted our relationship to go, but I would not let myself believe that it could. My mind was full of wishful, dangerous, scary thoughts painting a vivid masterpiece of what might be.

As time went on, my path continued to cross Beth's at activities involving the youth group, music, and the church softball team. I did not pursue her, at least not consciously. We just kept going our separate ways until one night we met face-to-face and could not continue on as before without one of us changing direction. That night, while walking in the woods together, Beth told me of her desires, and I told her of my past. After answering a year's worth of questions, we found the truth and were rocketed toward complete emotional intimacy, the colors of which were like fireworks, hot and spectacular. We did all the things that two young people in love would do. We got together as often as possible, sharing the deepest desires of our beings—emotionally, spiritually, physically. Yet whatever we did was shrouded in secrecy. I wanted to shout, "I have found the one!" I wanted more than anything for people to be happy for us. But despite all the joy, I knew they never would be. Beth completed the art masterpiece I had envisioned, yet put me in danger once again and my future in jeopardy.

By the fall of 1982, I knew I had to end my relationship with the alien. Although he would have been almost any woman's dream, to me whatever excitement had existed was long gone. I regretted the way I had treated him. He deserved a lot more than what I could give. As with my previous boyfriends, I again had the luxury of knowing for so long the breakup was coming that the actual moment of it did not faze me. Judging by his reaction, he seemed to have known it, too, and was relieved. We were both emancipated; he was free to find his future, and for me, finally able to say good-bye to commonplace, beige was gone forever.

I was still in love with Beth, maybe in love for the first time. I lived at home, and she attended the community college and lived with her parents, but in the evenings we were rarely apart. We still had our social connections with the youth group, to whom we simply appeared as two inseparable friends.

Sadly, constant concealment became as much a routine as brushing our teeth. In many ways I was right back where I had started. But somewhere in this sham of existence I knew God still wanted me to serve him. I could live out my life as a good example of a Christian at the bank, but I wanted to do more. I also knew that if God wanted me in his service he would have to show me what he had in mind.

CHAPTER 13

Calling to Missionary Work

IN THE FALL OF 1982 I NOT ONLY ENDED my relationship with the alien but had also graduated from college with a bachelor of science degree in Biblical Studies and a minor in Christian Education. My mother was proud. I had accomplished what I set out to do. I loved God, and I could not think of anything better to do than serve him in a full-time capacity.

I now realized the dream of having a pastor-husband was probably not in my future so I was going to have to find a job on my own. Teaching women and children was my only option, but that limited me to either securing a position at a large church or becoming an overseas missionary; both choices would have required relocating, which did not appeal to me. Nor did I know how to start finding a suitable job locally. I didn't feel I could use the job placement resources from college to help me since school officials knew of my past and might not give me a wholehearted recommendation. Frustrated, I began to think my choice of degrees had been foolish.

I told myself that if I found a job my relationship with Beth would have to stop, as a homosexual lifestyle could not coexist with my service to God. Yet I could not see my future without Beth. At times I was ready to surrender my dream of the ministry, but moments later I'd experience flickers of hope that lured me into thinking I just might be able to work in a church. I still felt that God was in control and had a plan for my life.

The option of serving God as an overseas missionary had first been presented to me at a young age. Some of my earliest memories had been of hearing the stories our church missionaries told about faraway places and strange customs. When they came home on furlough and spoke at Sunday services, I didn't doodle on my bulletin or make paper airplanes from the inserts; rather, I sat perched at the edge of my hardwood seat caught up in every word, my patent leather shoes dangling inches from the floor. Stories of forgiveness were interwoven with exciting tales of cannibalism, malaria, giant snakes, and miracles of healing or protection. Every account ended with how God worked miracles.

It was common practice in many evangelical churches like ours to reserve a portion of the budget for missions. When a person or couple got their calling, their first task was to join a mission organization that believed in the same theology and goals. The mission organization trained them and assisted them every step along the way. Most missionaries did not have paying jobs in the countries where they were going, so they depended on American Christians to assist with their expenses. From the early days of the church up through the 1980s, most missionaries were expected to be "lifers." If God called you, you went and stayed for life.

Getting called by God to do something does not necessarily mean hearing an audible voice but instead implies having an unmistakable certainty that God wants you to take action of some sort. It might start with an idea planted by something you read or heard about. The seed that is planted becomes rooted and grows until you have no doubt what is being asked of you. The call is usually accompanied by a peace that antidotes any fear of the endeavor. Christians I know who have departed for the rainforests of South America or Rwanda, or other mission destinations involving potential danger, have had no fear since God had called them.

Our Baptist church supported about ten missionary families. We were reminded to pray for them by the missionary board. This board was not a group of men in thin-lapeled black suits at a conference table but a six-by-five-foot corkboard with a world map containing photos of missionaries tacked to the places where they were serving. Some photos showed them in the jungles of Africa; others showed families posed in front of modest concrete block buildings that served as churches. No matter what part of the world they illustrated, all the images had two things in common: bad clothes and lots of children. What struck me especially was that the people in the photos on the missionary board were smiling, living in places beyond my sphere of knowledge, and exuding a spirit of adventure.

These missionaries also positively impacted my parents. Normally, both my parents were rather reclusive, having very little social life; but Don and Mary woke from their hibernation when the missionaries came to town. To them, missionaries were selfless individuals who deserved honor. Our family demonstrated our respect by inviting the visitors for supper. I thrived in their company. They had been somewhere. They loved God. I was glad they had been willing to go to places that sounded scary and had snakes.

At the age of about ten, I was sure I had heard God's call to the mission field while in church. I then went down to the altar and said, "Here I am Lord, send me," meaning it with all my heart. I was sure I would be called to Africa or some other faraway land, but as I became a teen I found I had no desire to leave our country, wanting instead to serve people in the United States. In my years at Bible college, I had developed a shameful haughtiness, seeing those who served overseas as less polished and effective than those who served at home. Still, I thought God might call one of the teens from church to serve in this capacity, so I wanted them to learn about this opportunity to serve.

One Saturday morning, several teens, a few other leaders, and I hopped on a bus destined for a missionary conference. There speakers from several missionary boards told us of ministering opportunities around the world. I sat silently praying that God would call one of the students I had brought to his mission field. God did call that day—but he called me. Toward the end of the afternoon when we were weary from hours of sitting, I had begun counting the minutes till closing when the final speaker suddenly grabbed my attention. It certainly wasn't his appearance that had drawn me in: even though he was pint-sized, his suit appeared to be two sizes too small, the cuffs of his white shirt sticking out four inches below the sleeves of his jacket. His pointy face was almost ratlike, and his hair was slicked back with so much hair cream you could see your face in it. But when he spoke of his passion to tell the world about Christ, I could feel each word directed at my heart. This man was from an organization that was not composed of stodgy older men sizing you up and making you pass countless personality tests to prove you were ready; nor was there any need to raise support from dozens of churches, or to reach a certain quota before you could go. This was short term, and the money needed was minimal because each person's work was subsidized by the sale of Bibles and Christian books that would stay in the hands of their purchasers long after they had been told about the good news.

That day I was called to be a missionary. Although shocked, I did not resist, for I was "in perfect peace" (Isaiah 26:3).

It was an ideal opportunity to serve, and I couldn't help but wonder if the distance from Beth would help me forget her. I thought that emotional immaturity may have been holding me back and that with God's help I could love a man after all. I didn't realize at the time that such thoughts were emanating from a mind subjected to weekly doses of church disapproval of homosexuality. I could not escape the fact that I would never be accepted as I was. To my Christian brothers and sisters, I was an outsider.

When I told Beth I had been called to serve as a missionary, she was upset but felt confident she could live during my time away knowing I would be home again in a year. She never spoke of breaking up, only of how difficult our time apart would be. However, in the back of my mind I was determined to see if this would lead to a permanent separation, hoping that, if that was God's desire for me, my urge to spend a lifetime with Beth would pass.

The few months between my decision and my departure were not uneventful. I made the necessary preparations, and the small amount of money I needed during the year of serving God abroad was pledged by my home church. Meanwhile, Beth and I enjoyed each minute we still had together in each other's arms. Life without one another seemed unimaginable, but we both tried to be brave despite the fact that I was leaving for adventure and she was being left behind.

One month before I was scheduled to leave, I was again reminded of the church's restrictive views and disapproval in a frightening way. The youth whom I had taught through high school began to come home from college. Being good Baptists, and with most of them still underage, we just had good clean fun together, going bowling or to the movies or out to eat, until one fateful night. I had heard about a family-type restaurant where patrons could eat dinner then dance to popular music, so I arranged for our group to go there. That evening we drank Coke, danced together, and laughed at each other's attempts to look cool, resulting in a memorable summer night shared by friends finding their way in the adult world.

However, while at work a few days later I got a call from the Christian education pastor at church, who oversaw the Sunday School and activities involving children. To have the Christian education pastor call me at work was not odd since I had interned with him, planning church programs while in college the previous year. I regarded him as a mentor and his family members as friends, having spent many hours dining joyfully together and sharing the common bonds of the ministry.

"Susan," he said, calling me by a name used only by people who do not know me, "you need to come to my house tonight. We have to discuss something." His words conveyed an element of cruelty, leaving me in dread regarding the nature of the call.

Struck with terror, I assumed he knew about Beth and that I was going to face round two of being kicked out and disgraced. The rest of the day I was in a fog of depression, believing I would spend the night groveling and apologizing.

That evening I fearfully walked up the concrete steps to the pastor's small Cape Cod–style house and was greeted by him and his wife, both bearing the grim expressions of people who had been given a loathsome task they wanted to put behind them as quickly as possible. I was escorted past the living room into their cramped study and asked to sit. Many times in the past we had relaxed in this room, playing games and sharing friendship. But today the pastor had positioned himself in a side chair while his wife sat at attention on the piano bench. He wore his everyday Mr. Rogers sweater, and she was still in her dress from work but had exchanged her pumps for a pair of large fluffy white slippers. The slippers, although glaringly out of place, seemed to be the only sign of normality in the room.

The pastor began, in a very businesslike tone, by saying that he had asked his wife to be there to listen, a message that, according to biblical teachings on conflict, suggested the meeting was to be about big trouble, making me more terrified. Interestingly, the biblical advice about conflict resolution is the opposite of typical human behavior. Most people avoid conflict by saying such things as, "It will blow over," burying their feelings, shutting down or staying away from potential conflict. All of this comes at a cost—loss of friendship and family, anger, shame, and bitterness. By contrast, biblical conflict solution is a head-on approach. The Bible says, "If your brother wrongs you, go to him" (Matthew 18:15). Heeding this advice clears the air and leads more often to forgiveness.

In my case, what was terrifying about the pastor's wife being there was that providing a witness for conflict resolution is step two according to biblical advice. The Bible advises: "If your brother doesn't hear you, take a witness, maybe then the two of you can restore the one that was harmed" (Matthew 18:16). Although I tried to act cool, my demeanor surely reflected my feelings of anxiety and guilt.

The pastor then bit his lip before saying, with a great sense of gravity, "It's been reported that you have been . . . dancing."

I exhaled with relief and joy, and immediately, somewhere between my intestines and belly button, a giggle began to form. Relief sprang from my chest with a burst of exhilarating joy. "Dancing?" I said. I could not help myself. The giggle that had formed came to my throat, and I tipped my head back in full, unabashed laughter.

My two former friends sat frozen, their faces reflecting shock and disgust. To them, this was no laughing matter since parents were concerned that I had taken their children to a restaurant to dance. For me, there was great relief that Beth and I were safe and I was not being accused of sleeping with one of the pastor's granddaughters. After I was able to calm down sufficiently to address the pastor's concerns, I had enough strength to challenge him about the ban on dancing. *After all*, I wondered, *what could be wrong with moving the body that God has given us?* Besides, our dancing that evening had not been lewd or seductive but more like an exercise class. "Where in the Bible does it say that people shouldn't dance?" I asked, laughing once again as a sense of freedom shot through my veins and nervous system. Appalled and dumbfounded, the pastor got up and mumbled something about letting the senior pastor know my thoughts. I drove away saddened, and sure I'd reached the beginning of the end of my association with this church.

In the minds of the church officials, I had committed something just short of a crime. They had wanted to discipline me, to set me straight. I could see it in their eyes and hear it in their voices, but the Bible did not back them up. I had slipped through an unintended exit. This time, the Bible itself had been my savior. With the scriptures as their authority, they had to obey its teachings. Romans 14 was my defense: "And everything that does not come of faith is sin," a verse that is interpreted to mean that in gray areas where the Bible does not state something is right or wrong, people must rely on their conscience for guidance. Thus if I did not think dancing was wrong, they could not nail my feet to the floor. But the episode with the Christian education pastor would not be their last attempt to discipline me. Hadn't I led college kids down a path toward debauchery? If they danced, what would be next?

Subsequently, the education pastor told the senior pastor about my reaction, and he asked to speak with me. I drove to the church on a weeknight feeling like a child who had been summoned to the principal's office. The massive brick building in the distance was quiet and dark; the only lights were those illuminating the path to my next brush with authority. I knocked and stepped into his spacious, well-appointed church office. His domain was still ablaze in the last rays of the summer evening. In the midst of this display of nature's glory stood the senior pastor, a stern man in his late sixties with snow-white hair. His thick glasses magnified his eyes and hung on his oddly shaped nose. I was scared, but somehow this was different from meeting with the Christian education pastor. I had come to the sensible conclusion that being the ringleader against the church's policy of no dancing had probably not been a smart choice, especially since, given my past, church officials could be looking for something to drive me from the church. But I was resolved not to let them bully me.

The senior pastor sat behind his enormous cherry-wood desk and motioned for me to take a seat in front of him. Speaking in short staccato sentences, he reported what the church education director had told him about our conversation. Although he directed his words toward me with a cold, authoritative tone, I could hear his heart shouting at me, "Troublemaker, woman in a man's world, you are no good." The sentences turned to paragraphs before he wound down to a close. Just like his best sermons, this teaching had to have a take-away thought, something that would cause me to mull over the sin I had committed. His posture changed as he moved closer to the desk, folded his hands in businesslike reverence, and said, "When the elder board heard about your dancing, they were going to pull your support for the mission field, but we believe you really love God, so we have decided to still let you go." This was the take-away thought to mull over. He had preached his sermon of judgment and discipline, and I saw a glimmer of triumph in his eyes. With this, combined with his declaration that dancing and loving God were in opposition, he had succeeded in undermining my devotion to his church. Then and there I decided I would go to the mission field but never come back to this place I had called home.

CHAPTER 14

Irish Temptation

FOR THE FIRST WEEK OF MISSION TRAINING before traveling to Belgium for orientation, I gathered with other young people from all over the country at a large church in Canton, Ohio. The week was designed for us to understand how the organization was structured, as well as to spend time worshiping to prepare our hearts for service. The first two days of new sights, sounds, and education distracted me from the distance between Beth and myself. But as the week went on, the agonizing truth that I would not see her for a year began to set in. I did everything in my power to keep my mind busy, but I felt empty without her. Our brief telephone conversations told me two things: she would not stand in the way of what God was calling me to do and she seemed to be shrinking inside from a combination of grief and yearning.

From Ohio, most people in our mission training went directly to New York, to fly to Belgium, but I had to see Beth one more time before leaving the country. After traveling all night by bus and train, I ran excitedly through the train station until I finally reached the escalator that would carry me to the bottom, where I knew Beth would be waiting, smiling, loving me. I had no thoughts about the pain that would come the next day. I just needed to be with her, my best friend and my love.

The clock seemed to move in double time that last day, and before we knew it the time had come to part once more. My mother, my sister, and Beth took me to JFK Airport to see me off. My mother and sister had to know that this was much more than friends saying good-bye, but they didn't acknowledge our pain. For me, somehow the excitement of doing God's calling outweighed the torture of our separation.

Over the next ten days in Brussels, amidst jet lag and culture shock we split into teams and received our assignments for the summer. The building where we slept, worshiped, and learned was huge, encompassing several acres and three or four stories of mostly concrete block and rows and rows of windows, enough space to house the thousands who had come. The furnishings were modest at best, sort of a cross between a campground and a twelfth-century monastery, but we did not care, so excited were we about our missionary experience to come.

The women's dorms constituted an entire wing with row after row of about twenty wooden cots each. A global milieu, my row alone held young women from Germany, Canada, South Africa, England, and Australia. We saw our differences and discovered our commonalities. Most of all, we had our shared love of Jesus and what he had done for us. Our goal was to tell others of his love, not to force it on them but to offer it.

Three things especially stand out about those ten days: bathing, hazelnut spread, and worship. I could not help but notice the differences in bathing customs among my row mates. The German women would stand buck naked in front of the sinks filled with warm water, using their washcloths with reckless abandon to scrub each part of their body as if no part was private. By contrast, the women from the United States would act as if their bodies were different from those of the rest of the female population of the universe, filling the sink and then carefully holding their towels in front of them while giving their private parts a little swish with a washcloth. Some girls would run back and forth from the sink to lavatory stalls, where they would wash in their own private hideaways. By the end of the first week, sanity prevailed when quite a few uptight Americans realized that the straightforward German method made the most sense and that a good scrub among friends is a terrific way to start the day.

After our daily washing, we went to the cafeteria for a European breakfast. For most of the participants, there was nothing unusual about the breakfast offerings, but the Americans weren't sure what they were eating. The strange jellied lunchmeats, dried fish (eyeballs included), and other unidentifiable foods were hard for us to eat. Plus, there was bread but no peanut butter, which we Americans craved. The Europeans, laughing at our strange yearnings, instead offered us a jar of brownish black paste. Through sign language and a lot of trust, we cautiously smelled it, licked it . . . and loved it. Chocolate hazelnut spread helped us quickly forget about peanut butter.

The cultural differences among the new missionaries were ultimately eclipsed by the unity we experienced in worship sessions during orientation. A tent had been erected on the grounds for worship and educational gatherings. There, individuals from all the nations sat intermingled but sang in their native languages accompanied by instruments played by many diverse, talented participants. The improvised orchestra, made up of people of various nations and cultures, made me feel like I was witnessing the world uniting in praise to God. It was a celebration of the beauty of our differences and similarities for the glory of the God we loved.

By the end of the ten days, we had been separated into groups and assigned to a country for the summer. My group, bound for Ireland, was composed of six people—three women from the United States; one man from Scotland; one man from Canada; and our team leader, Andrew, from England. Upon arriving in Ireland, we were to work with two churches, one located in Limerick and the other in Cork.

After crossing the sea from the mainland to England, we boarded the ferry for Ireland. I sat on the upper deck surveying the beauty of the Irish passengers returning home with their families, their shiny brown-black hair, their blue eyes, the sprinkle of freckles across their pale faces. I thought to myself, *How beautiful these people are!* and then realized that just as God had placed an attraction in the heart of every missionary before me for the people they served, he had done the same for me. I had not chosen Ireland; God had chosen it for me.

Without a language barrier, we could jump right into our program. It turned out that the only real language barrier we had was with our Scottish teammate, who was from Glasgow and whose Scottish accent kept us from understanding almost everything he said. It got so bad the guy had to sing everything he wanted to say, as singing slowed down his speech enough that we could decipher his words. Although perhaps frustrating for him, these antics were a constant source of laughter for us.

Upon beginning our missionary activities, every day we went from house to house to talk to people, encouraging them to come to Bible studies, selling them Bibles, telling Bible stories to the children of the itinerant gypsies who still roamed Ireland's countryside, and performing skits in the streets of Limerick. As part of our orientation, we were reminded that Ireland was a very religious country and the church was a deeply ingrained part of people's lives. They were baptized in the church, confirmed in the church, married in the church, and then had their funerals in the church. But we wanted them also to know that God wished to be a part of their everyday lives, not just on the specified holy days. I don't know if we made a difference. Our job was to try; God had to do the rest.

Beth was still in my mind, but there was little time to think about how much I missed her. I wrote to her at least once a week, yet due to the miles between us, the letters went from hot to lukewarm, eventually having the tone of friendship. I wondered whether the distance between us was indeed working to cool our relationship and if God was making me ready to love a man.

The summer rushed by, after which I said good-bye to my team and headed back to Brussels for my next assignment. I could have gone many places, but lacking knowledge of any language other than English I signed up for Ireland again.

This time Ireland was much different. I did not have my teammates to buffer me. I traveled from Brussels to Ireland by myself, feeling like a Livingston or Elliott setting out on my own with God, to tell others about the good news. My assignment for the next ten months was to work in a bookstore in downtown Dublin that was owned and operated by the mission, just blocks from Trinity College.

My roommate, Catherine, a woman from England, was wonderful, and we hit it off immediately. We weren't exactly soulmates, but for two people thrown together who grew up an ocean apart we got along spectacularly. She loved to laugh, and I loved to make people laugh so my American invasion was taken in stride. Catherine's claim to fame was her prosthetic arm. She had been born with an arm only down to her elbow, a malady with which she was completely comfortable. Nothing pleased her more than to be asked to "lend a hand." More than once I would see her hand her arm to an unsuspecting person or pass it through a crowd to her intended target. Her habit of leaving it around the apartment was unnerving, but I quickly grew accustomed to her dark sense of humor.

We lived on the second floor of a stately Victorian mansion located in a row of similar homes that stood as sentinels overlooking Dublin Bay, the kind of street pictured in postcards. Our house seemed to have a life of its own, holding on to its age with its faded curtains and creaking floors. Everything about it was spacious, from the windows to the impressive rooms and wide entrance. But this mansion came with drawbacks. For one thing, it had no hot running water or heat. In addition, we had to get past the miserable old landlady who lived on the first floor. This challenge required us to come in the massive white wooden front door, tiptoe across a threadbare Oriental rug, and immediately shut the door to the upstairs. Then we climbed the wooden staircase knowing we were safe for one more day from the prying eyes of the nosy woman below.

I took the first of these drawbacks in stride. Each morning, I would heat the electric kettle full of water and use the old German method to bathe from head to toe using the bathroom sink. Each Thursday, I would put a coin in the hot water heater to heat water for a bath. Although it produced only an inch of water, I always seemed to make it work. Enduring the winter with no heat was considerably more difficult. I would use the electric heater while awake, but the 1930s wiring made it too scary to leave on while I slept. The only way I could keep warm at night was to wear gloves and cocoon myself in a heavy, hooded sweatshirt with the drawstring pulled tight, leaving only a small circle so my nose and mouth could get air. Enveloped in my chrysalis, I would stay nuzzled in this world of warmth until morning.

My family wrote often, marveling at my lack of creature comforts. But somehow I just rolled with the circumstances, content in my belief that I was where God wanted me to be.

I spent days working at the bookstore with Catherine and the two other members of our team, each from a different country and each with their own peculiarity. There was Catherine, the English armless wonder; Patrick, the effeminate, giggling Irishman; Sue, the outgoing, loud American; and David, the bookish Welsh team leader. But none of us let these peculiarities overshadow our common interest—we all loved the same Jesus.

On my days off, I explored Dublin and spent time with friends I had met at church. Patrick was the first to invite me to his church, a congregation of the Brethren denomination that met in the home of one of the leaders. They were warm and welcoming to me, and would often invite me to dinner.

My missionary term was going well until Catherine announced that she would be leaving because she had an opportunity to go to Rwanda. She knew it was dangerous, but she also realized the great need for the people of Rwanda to hear about God's love. Within a few months, she was gone and I was left alone in the mansion.

Living alone in a foreign country did not frighten me, but without being accountable to another missionary I soon compromised my calling in the mission field and brought shame to myself and my God. The woman's name was Colleen, and I had met her six months earlier in Cork. It was a Sunday morning, and a few of us from the team were standing on the sidewalk in downtown Cork talking before going into church. We knew that if we lingered any longer we would be late, but we couldn't help ourselves. All was relatively quiet, and the sun was making a rare appearance, its brilliant light transforming this portion of the Emerald Isle to the fairyland of legends. Then, as we reluctantly headed to the church the rumbling sound of a motorcycle caught our attention. The black motorcycle, moving down the street and slowing to a purr as it entered an empty parking space beside us, was wrapped with the frame of a large woman. The helmet she wore accented the powerful command she had over her machine. In the morning sun, the polished chrome glinted as she dismounted.

My friends continued toward the church, but I wasn't about to go anywhere. My eyes were glued to the helmet, eager to see what was underneath it. My heart skipped a beat as I thought, *Strong screaming gay Irish chick.* Her first impression scored a ten with me and gave me a reason to break out my old smirk. But the smirk quickly turned to surprise as this robust temptation straightened her leather and walked past me into the church, making me sure this was going to be an interesting service.

I couldn't have had more than two conversations with Colleen while in Cork those six weeks. But any time we were in the same room we kept our eyes on each other. I wondered if she was attracted to me because of some gaydar frequency or just interested in a new friend.

Four months later she suddenly called, asking if she could spend a weekend with me in Dublin, no doubt having received my phone number from a church member. I had not thought much about her, but hearing her voice I realized I was still intrigued by this motorcycle mama. I asked myself, *Why, after all these months, did Colleen decide to call?* Yet even though I had only spent a limited time with her, I was eager for her to arrive, thinking it would be nice to have another woman around to talk to. Was I being honest with myself about where a friendship with her might lead? Absolutely not.

When she stood at the bottom of the wide exterior staircase leading to the mansion, I was struck by the fact that there was a coyness about her smile, characteristic of both sheep and wolf—her sheepishness probably due to fear of rejection and her wolfishness because of her seeming readiness to pounce at the slightest signal of my availability. Once alone in the mansion together, it was a setup for disaster. We had wine with dinner, and talked. Sometime during the evening I made a conscious decision— the wolf became the prey.

Although our intimate encounter was exciting, it had occurred purely out of sexual desire. I knew it had been wrong as there was no real love between us. I wondered why a trusted servant of God, who had a higher calling than to be sexually needy and act on it, would do such a thing. I had been unable to make it through one year without getting into this sort of trouble again.

The fact was that Beth had faded. I was alone and wanted intimacy, and I had a fling for fun. I was ashamed of myself. I was still telling Beth that I loved her, although I certainly wasn't going to tell her about Colleen. I told Colleen that I was not sure about Beth and me. Colleen had fallen for me; I cared for her, but those feelings were nothing compared to how I felt about Beth.

Following this time together, the four-hour distance between Colleen and me, as well as our lack of finances, kept us apart. We spent only two other weekends together, six days total. Still, if I had known how much pain those nights of foolish indiscretion would later cause and how they would affect my future, I would never have allowed Colleen to stay that first weekend. We reap what we sow. In my case, the harvest came a few years later.

The highlights of the rest of my time in Ireland were two separate visits—one from my mother and the other from Beth. I was proud of my mother for not allowing her usual fears of getting hopelessly lost prevent her from visiting. I excitedly awaited her at the airport, eager to show her my new world. Having reverted to my "take care of her" mode, I was planning to be her tour guide, the one responsible for the logistics of her visit to the Emerald Isle. I had hardly said hello when the fun began. Even though my grandmother's last name was Murphy, I had never realized how Irish my mother looked. I expected to wait an hour or more as she passed through customs, but within minutes she appeared. When I asked her what happened in customs, she said she had gotten in the visitor's line but a customs officer had waved her through, welcoming her home. We laughed about her Irish roots as time after time someone would mistake her for a local, asking her for directions.

We spent a week traveling by car, seeing the beautiful rugged green vistas of the Irish countryside but sharing few words. In a letter before her arrival she had told me she was proud of me for being a missionary. Her words of praise, which were only written, were scarce and cheerless. She didn't know of my fall; nor did she know I was still in love with Beth. Had she known, I would have been forced to endure her disappointment for she never supported who I really was. Like stinging barbs, her disapproval was never far from my thoughts. I could not be what she wanted; I was going to have to find my way without her approval.

Later, Beth arrived for a visit. She had worked out a way to come see me and help with the mission short-term, doing things for which we had no time, such as sprucing up the bookstore, cleaning, painting, and other maintenance. I should have been over the moon to have her visit, but instead I was conflicted about my love for her and my future with the church. I had settled into missionary life and was contemplating serving in Ireland permanently. I was also still upset about my encounters with Colleen. So when Beth and I talked before she arrived, we decided we would be just friends.

As Beth walked off the plane, it was apparent that we were not the same people who had parted. She was much heavier, worn down from our time apart, and looking like the weight of the world had been upon her shoulders. I was thinner and more mature, having been very active in my new life of adventure. Nevertheless, we set out to discover where our lives might still intersect. It didn't take long. Our feelings of love for each other soon came rushing back, and within days we were where we had left off.

But now I knew I wanted to spend a lifetime with her. I had asked God to take the interest in women from my life, and he hadn't. I had failed miserably at resisting temptation with Colleen. However, Beth was different. My relationship with Beth was not about lust; it was was about a loving partnership, a marriage of two hearts forever. The church had told me the scriptures said this was wrong, but instead of being convinced of the truth of these assertions, I had reached a new and dangerous conclusion: if my feelings for Beth were wrong, I didn't care.

I was now on a path of quiet rebellion. I knew it was a "fearful thing to fall into the hands of the living God" (Hebrews 10:31), but I felt I would have to take my chances. I agonized over whether I was directly going against God's will for my life and told myself that if I was, God was going to have to change my heart to help me to know it was wrong. I knew I had free will, yet I was giving it all to God, including my desires. He had to guide me to the right path. If I was wrong, he could take my life. I could not stand the torture of uncertainty any longer. When my missionary term was over, I needed to move forward in life with the person I loved.

CHAPTER 15

Seeing the World and Settling Down

A FEW MONTHS AFTER HER FIRST TRIP TO IRELAND, Beth returned, and we took a whirlwind tour of Europe. The dollar was strong, so we knew our meager funds would go a long way provided we were careful about expenditures. We discovered that the full Irish breakfast of potatoes, bacon, eggs, and toast was enough for two meals. We ate the potatoes and eggs for breakfast and saved our bacon and toast for the makings of a hardy lunch. We hitchhiked through Northern Ireland; we sunned ourselves on the beaches of Nice; we saw the Swiss Alps in their splendor, enjoying the differences of each surrounding country. Every new country brought fresh beauty to our eyes and confidence to our hearts. Starting out as two wide-eyed young women in awe, we were ushered into maturity, trusting that if we could travel together around Europe with such enjoyment, once back home we would be ready for the new adventure called adult life together.

When I returned to the United States after our European tour, instead of moving back in with my mother I accepted an invitation from Beth's family, who offered to give me a room of my own in exchange for minimal rent. I am not sure why they took me in. They believed homosexuality was a sin. They would not have approved of sex in their home outside the confines of marriage. Knowing how much Beth had missed me, maybe they wanted to see her happy again. Or perhaps they were simply naive, as a lesbian relationship was unheard of in the Christian community at the time. Regardless of the reason, they were generous and loving and didn't seem to notice or be concerned about the fact that Beth and I shared a bed each night. Had they questioned us, some lame excuse about the terrible mattress was all it would have taken to satisfy them. Having come from a home where my actions had been constantly watched and assessed, this amazed me. It was the perfect setup, and the fact that they didn't know I considered them my in-laws was mute. They were my relatives, for I'd become as fond of them as if they were my own.

My job at the bank was waiting for me upon my return, and I was glad to be employed. Then after a few months, I was approached by a man named Sean O'Malley, manager of the real estate company that shared the building with the bank. An odd-looking man of Irish descent, overly tall with a lanky gait, black hair, light skin, and protruding front teeth, he said, "You look like you have a brain in your head. Would you like a job as an office administrator?" He offered me a huge salary increase, and I immediately said yes, two weeks later embarking on a new career that seemed to come out of the blue but which I was convinced had been sent by God through the protruding lips of an Irishman. By the time Beth graduated from college with a teaching degree in physical education, I had begun to climb the ladder in real estate. We knew it was time to get our own apartment and start our lives together.

Consequently, we moved to a town thirty minutes from where our parents lived to a fabulous apartment that had originally been part of an old house. It was drafty but had lots of room, including a wonderful covered back porch. We had picked this town for two reasons: my sister had lived there, so I knew about the area, and we had heard of a church there that could perhaps be our new spiritual home.

The new church we attended had been established by a humble man who, very different from the pastor of our former church, realized he had faults and considered himself a sinner saved by God's grace. The church members were former motorcycle gang members he had led to Christ. As soon as we started attending this church, we fell in love with it. This was no white bread environment; these were folks who had been around the block and knew what God could do for them. Communion was given in shorts and flip-flops; the pastor openly admitted to his shortcomings; the congregants were not clean or polished, only forgiven.

Although these new Christians had come from a world of drugs, sex, and every other vice imaginable, Beth and I instinctively knew that even here the homosexual lifestyle was considered taboo, so to be accepted we presented ourselves as roommates. Immersing ourselves in the culture of our new church, I quickly became involved with the youth group, while Beth added her beautiful voice and guitar playing to the Sunday worship service.

The youth group in this church was nothing like the one in our previous church, where most families had brought their children from a young age and they grew up knowing how they were expected to act and how to respect the leadership. Here the parents had just found God for themselves, and their teens, having never before been to church, didn't know the Bible and felt they had been dragged to a place their parents now considered their new life. These young hellions showed no respect for the leadership. Their faces had a "go ahead and try to change me" look. They wore chips on their shoulders as badges of honor.

One day soon after I had become involved with the youth group, the youth pastor announced that we would be having an autumn dance. As the words came out of his mouth, I experienced free-falling culture shock. When the big night came, instead of enjoying the freedom of dancing I spent the evening seesawing between amusement and apprehension. I watched incredulously as the youth pastor encouraged the teens to show off their best moves. Consciously I knew it was good clean fun, but I could not shake the feeling that somehow doom was just a few days and a phone call away. This time, the phone didn't ring—only freedom chimed as my past and its rules began to unravel from the hold they had on my life.

As much as I wanted to help, I soon determined that I was not suited for this youth group. I didn't know how to interact with the teens, and I couldn't seem to reach them. Maybe I was not willing to go the extra mile with them while they were being disrespectful toward me and each other. In any case, I quit the leadership and looked for other ways to serve.

One Sunday morning during church, Beth whispered an idea to me that must have been sent from heaven—a suggestion that we start a women's softball team. With anticipation of being on the field again, I sprang into action. It took only a couple of weeks to find out that there were plenty of ex-softball players in the congregation, so after a few phone calls to neighboring churches, we formed a team and joined a church league. Beth and I not only developed the team but also led the practices.

By the end of our team's second year in the league, we were beating the opposition with such regularity that we needed a more competitive atmosphere, so we joined the women's township league, which was composed of six teams sponsored by four bars, an auto parts store, and a church. Initially, we weren't sure if we were good enough. This new league would be a huge leap into the world of beer drinking, large-biceped women who could—and most likely would—tear us God-loving wimps apart. To meet their Goliaths, we puny Davids were going to have to fight. In fact, we started our practice so early in the season that the frozen ground crunched beneath our cleats. We were prepared for battle, and when the season began our slingshots were ready.

We competed against a new team each week, and invariably our opponents would spit and stare in our direction from their side of the field, scrutinizing us as we took our turn warming up. They would glare as we gathered for prayer behind our chain-link dugout fence, praying for protection. Our goal was to share our faith through our words and actions, but as we faced each new team of Goliaths we laughed at having volunteered for such abuse.

Miraculously, we experienced win after win throughout the season. We ended up as champions—not only for that year but for many more to come. With me playing first base and coaching and Beth as one of the heavy hitters, we were as much a team on the field as off.

Softball was a marvelous diversion, but I also wanted to be involved with a ministry again. Realizing our new church had Sunday School but no other program for elementary school children, I thought of developing a Kid's Club. I told the pastors about my idea, and they gave Beth and me the go-ahead to establish one. So Beth and I became partners in yet another endeavor. I got volunteers to help and signed on with the national association. Beth contributed her skills with games and music. Others brought their own skills and willingness to serve. God blessed as the attendance rose each week. In six years, our Kid's Club grew from fifteen to over eighty children each week. Watching their faces as we sang corny songs was a delight. Seeing them smile as we played games and made weekly crafts brought a welcome satisfaction. Pointing them to God gave us joy.

Beth and I had found our place in this new church. Yet we lived in fear, wondering if someone would discover our homosexual lifestyle. If we were found out, we agreed, we had no choice but to lie since no one would understand or condone our behavior. Secretly, however, we hoped that if our lifestyle were discovered, our love for the church and our work in service to God would count for something. We imagined that the church leadership and members would see how our ministries flourished and come to the conclusion that God had blessed our relationship. We dreamed of a response of grace because we loved each other and God, and they would surely see that we were part of their family. We knew our optimism was a fantasy; fear kept us under a veil of secrecy, which, if lifted, would reveal the devastating truth.

CHAPTER 16

The Secret Sisterhood

DESPITE OUR NEED TO SUPPRESS THE TRUTH about our homosexual relationship, without warning Beth and I found unspoken support from a group of women we called the Secret Sisterhood. For the previous nine years, except for revealing our secret to my sister Joyce, whom I considered my confidant and truest friend, and a few non-church friends Beth and I remained as closeted as hangers that never saw the light of day. In all those years, Beth's parents had remained silent about our relationship, although I'd been invited to every family function and had a permanent place in their lives. My mother, having been told about my sexual orientation years before and having watched Beth and me as an inseparable couple, was now sure of the type of relationship we shared. She spoke of her concerns only when her emotions reached the level of a volcanic eruption, whereupon she'd proclaim that our sin would result in damnation. I was undaunted by my mother's feelings, certain that God was in charge of my fate and it was only him that I needed to please.

Beth and I were very much in love, and, as it turned out, we were not alone. In the natural course of life, we had made friends during our church activities, especially the softball team and the Kid's Club. It didn't take long to notice some common denominators: most of our friends were women in their twenties who had professional jobs and seldom dated. Even though no words were ever shared in our siege of fear, members of this Secret Sisterhood silently presumed one another's sexual preference. Some were not ready to embrace the truth about their sexuality. Others had taken a hard look at their homosexuality and had vowed to fight it. Still others had accepted it. But as far as Beth and I knew, no one else had dared to take a life partner. Although the others did not ask us about our relationship, we dreaded the day they might. Fortunately, in the world of our sisterhood there was an unspoken pact of safety.

Members of the Secret Sisterhood sometimes dated because they thought they should, perhaps believing that the next date would be a man they could truly love. But most or all of them knew that dating was our way of throwing the world off our trail so others wouldn't think we were gay.

Actually, when members of the Secret Sisterhood dated problems would often surface. The guy might be cute or nice, so the woman would see him again. The thought of crossing over to the side of "the accepted ones" might entice her as she wondered if her former belief about her sexual orientation had been wrong. This could be reinforced when people at church said things like, "You two make such a cute couple." The dating might continue, maybe even for a year. But then the internal dying would begin, and the woman's emotional brakes would go on. These brakes did not go on because the woman found out the man had another girlfriend or was an ax murderer but because he called too much, chewed too loudly, or liked dogs while the woman liked cats. The woman would then make excuses, seeing those obstacles to love as insurmountable, while such an-noyances would never get in the way of true love. Members of the Secret Sisterhood would understand the truth about why the brakes had been applied—that one more sister had ended her quest to date because of lack of emotional connection and returned to the safety of the Secret Sisterhood.

Early in our relationship, Beth and I had also tried dating men. If we were asked on a date, we went, but we did not pursue men, doing our best to throw the watching eyes at church off our trails. Although we deeply loved each other, we did not believe we had what was best for us. We had been taught that men and women were built to complement each other and that two women could never fulfill each other's deepest needs to grow into the people God intended them to be. I dated a giant man from work, while Beth dated a handsome man from church. Both relationships ending with our respective brakes fully applied. For me, this happened when I compared the man to Beth. How cruel this was to the men, whom we'd allowed to spend money on us. How confused they must have felt when we kissed them good night and said good-bye forever. How delighted we were to come home to the warmth of the one we loved.

CHAPTER 17

Love Lost

WITH A STEADY INCOME AND BETH TEACHING FULL-TIME, we started to look at some of the houses I'd read about daily in the real estate business and soon purchased a little townhouse we loved. Now our lives were in a groove as we balanced our time between work, activities with friends and family, church, Kid's Club, and softball. We were living the freedom of a young adult life with few cares and a fair amount of fun.

We endured the occasional church service when homosexuality was spoken of as a sin. The pastor might say the word *homosexual* in passing, making it one point of many in an hour-long sermon, but it would be as if no other words had passed his lips. Our hearts would jolt and our palms would sweat, but we managed our anxiety and fear. We knew how the church felt—it was us against the world. Even so, we believed we were right in our convictions because our love was strong.

But one Sunday afternoon on the way home from church, this relative stability and tranquility in our lives began to crumble. We stopped to do our food shopping, and Beth asked if we could have lunch at the grill in the store. We sat on the round, padded aluminum stools, perched side by side like two birds waiting for our meal to arrive. Suddenly Beth turned toward me, her relaxed Sunday afternoon demeanor replaced by a look of defeat. "I can't do this anymore," she declared. "Can't do what anymore?" I asked. "I can't live like this," she confessed. Her words stung like an electric shock, stunning my every nerve ending to attention. My impulses screamed, "Warning," but my mind could not take in the message relayed by the one I loved. I wondered if she was thinking that our lifestyle was wrong or that she could not live with the constant unspoken opposition from our church and family. Yet I was afraid to ask any more questions. I simply said, "Please don't leave me." The rest of that afternoon was darkened by a heavy cloud of sadness. But by the next morning, the statement had faded, and everything returned to normal. Beth never uttered her proclamation again.

Soon, though, another event shook our world. After returning from Ireland, I had confessed to Beth my indiscretions with Colleen. She was not happy about it but forgave me with no further mention of it until I received a letter from Colleen. The lack of employment opportunities in Ireland was dire, and Colleen was asking me for sponsorship so she could come work in the United States. Sponsoring Colleen would require letting her stay with us at least until she got on her feet, and Beth wasn't sure she wanted this ex-lover in our house. Nor was she convinced that we could trust her with our secret. I felt stable in my relationship with Beth and was sure we could trust Colleen since she was one of us. I knew Colleen would work hard and felt that if I could help her, I should. Reluctantly, Beth agreed, and I filled out the paperwork to complete the sponsorship.

After eight months, I left for JFK Airport to pick up Colleen, but the Colleen who arrived wasn't the same large-framed woman who had once been my leather fantasy. This woman had the same coy smile, the same quick wit, but she wore smaller jeans and had a new air of confidence, making me think that Colleen might be seeking something more than a new job.

The living arrangements worked out nicely for six months. Colleen stayed in "Beth's room." In many gay relationships, bedrooms are a decoy, and ours was no exception. Just because Beth did not sleep in her room did not make it any less her room. We got an extra bureau for Colleen, and she seemed to feel at home instantly. I was soon able to get her an interview for an office administrator position in my company. She landed the job, and I was told she did fine work. Without a car, our life became hers as we did our best to introduce her at church and help her find her way in her new surroundings.

All seemed to be going well, but there were two fleeting telltale signs of trouble that should have alarmed me. One sign was Colleen's dramatic weight loss, which made me suspicious. She wanted me back. To ease my concern, I told myself that she was coming to a new country and had probably lost weight to make a good impression job seeking.

The other sign was her odd response to seeing Beth and me together in bed one evening. Beth and I were lying in bed in our pajamas reading before turning out the light for the night. Colleen, who was a typical Irish night owl, was still up and wanted to ask us a question. She politely knocked on the door, and we told her to come in. She remained in the doorway leaning against the jam, maintaining respect for our private space. Suddenly expressions of acknowledgment, jealousy, and hatred passed over her face in quick succession, which surprised and frightened me. I wondered why the sight of us lying in bed had caused such an intense reaction since Colleen already knew we shared a bed. I could only conclude that the truth had crashed down around her. The weight loss had been for nothing; leaving her country had been for nothing; I loved her as a friend and nothing more.

After Colleen had been with us for several months, as any good houseguest she found a way to not overstay her welcome. By now she had a job and a car and was ready to find a place of her own. We saw her at church and a few nights each week, but our lives naturally drifted back to our own activities and interests.

A few months later, an encounter with a second woman from my past created additional stress in my life with Beth. In the early 1990s, my latest promotion moved me from the real estate branch of the business into the title insurance department. The staff worked well together, and when our performance surpassed company goals we were rewarded with a Florida vacation. I hadn't been to Florida since my disgrace at the Bible college, and my thoughts turned to Lisa, wondering where she was, what she was doing, and if I should see her one more time for closure.

Even though I was apprehensive, I finally contacted Lisa, who was shocked to hear from me. She had graduated from Bible college and then returned to the gay lifestyle. We both had mates and were happy, but we decided it would be good to see each other. As usual, I was playing with fire.

On our second night in Florida I announced to my co-workers that I was meeting an old college friend. I had imagined our rendezvous as a Peyton Place soap opera drama of being lost in her eyes and riding into the Florida sunset together like we should have done so many years earlier. I had to know if what I had lost had been real and important, but I had no idea what I would do if it was. My anticipation was palpable; my heart was beating out of my chest. It was something out of a dream. All the objects around me seemed suddenly fuzzy. As I entered the little Italian restaurant where we had agreed to meet, I saw Lisa sitting in a dimly lit corner waiting, her dark hair lying perfectly over the side of her face. When she turned to greet me, I could see her face was still aglow with the tender spirit I remembered, her navy eyes still lighting her round innocent face. So much had been lost for the chance to be together that raw feelings of anguish colored our meeting. Although our conversation was idle, we held hands in full view of the other diners. We did not care what they thought; our hands had been ripped apart many years before, and now we were finding healing in each other's touch. A walk on the beach after dinner brought us full circle. The ocean breeze, the moonlit night, and the chill in the air made us find shelter in the cloth awning of a wooden chaise. Awkwardly, Lisa reached out to me for a tentative kiss, and in a moment we had our answer: this was a vain pursuit, a secret rendezvous with no spark or desire. The pain of our separation and years of being apart had dulled our attraction. It might have been wrong to meet Lisa without Beth's knowledge, but it was good to have confirmation once again that Beth was the one for my life. My love renewed, I anticipated going home to reunite with Beth and felt lucky that she was waiting for me.

Ironically, I was soon to experience loss rather than a comfortable reunion. When Beth picked me up at the airport late in the evening, my joy was met by sorrow on her countenance. I could see her eyes had sunken from her tears. Her steps were forced, her shoulders slumping from distress, her mouth slack. I ran to her, asking what had happened. She said she wanted to save it for the morning, but I persisted. Finally, she confessed, "The church found out, and I am leaving you." She hugged me, but her embrace was cold.

I writhed in spasms of emotional pain knowing the church was not forcing her to leave me, that this had been her choice. I begged her to tell me the details, yet at first she could barely speak, fearing my reaction.

Finally, Beth told me that Jeri, a woman whom Beth had sung with during worship services and a peripheral member of the Secret Sisterhood, had recently decided that her homosexual behavior was wrong and was working toward ridding it from her life. She had recently joined the staff of one of the ministries to help transform gay people to a heterosexual lifestyle, believing that it was her duty to set the captives free. Jeri felt sure that Beth and I were living in an unhealthy situation and needed to be confronted. But it had not been Jeri who confronted Beth; instead, Jeri had committed a taboo of biblical advice for conflict resolution by going to a third party. Her excuse was that she believed Beth would not tell her the truth. The third party was Colleen, whom she felt had to know the truth since she had lived with us for many months. Colleen had quickly and confidently confirmed what Jeri had suspected. With the proof Colleen had offered, Jeri had then gone to Beth. Thus Beth's fears about

Colleen's trustworthiness had been realized, and jealousy had found an outlet. I was finally reaping what I had sown. In a moment, my world had crumbled, blindsided by abandonment.

Beth mumbled, "You should have known. I told you." In my emotional coma, I scanned my memories of our life together, but other than Beth's one statement during the Sunday afternoon a long time before, there had been no warning about the possibility of these developments. Anger rose from my empty chest, but I did not know whether I should be angry with myself or with Beth.

I realized that Beth must have been waiting for someone to release her from the bondage of being a social outcast. There was no debate when I pressed her for an explanation. But I had questions about her decision: Was she leaving because God had told her our relationship was wrong or because she could no longer stand the double life we led? In any case, I couldn't blame her. We were two very different people who had sat through a lifetime of weekly indoctrination. Countless sermons had been delivered as truth by those we respected. But I had learned to question while she had been taught to follow. I still struggled with the church's doctrine on homosexuality; I was also starting to come to grips with the fact that the church's teaching went against everything I knew in my heart to be true. I could only speculate that Beth believed the church's teaching and it was this doctrine, coupled with the experience of being in social exile, that had driven her decision to leave. The choice of hiding our love or being excommunicated had been too much to bear. She had seen her chance to no longer live deceptively or be an outcast.

The next few weeks were a blur of the necessary. Sleeping and work were my salvation from constant pain. Eating became a thing of the past. I simply put one foot in front of the other in mindless routine. The church elders became everyday parts of our lives. To Beth, these men were welcomed guests, invited participants in the transformation to conformity she was ready to embrace. To me, they highlighted the chasm I felt between church doctrine about homosexuality and my inner feelings of love, which I still could not believe were at odds with true religious tenets.

The church elders advised us of the immediate measures needing to be taken. First, one of us had to move out. Whether it was out of guilt or ease, Beth quickly decided to be the one to go. Within forty-eight hours of her proclamation, she had packed her bags and was gone. The second measure to be taken was for us not to speak to or see each other. Not knowing where Beth was living facilitated the severing of all ties between us.

I sat alone staring at the walls of the house we used to share. I had believed there would be a lifetime of love ahead of me; now thoughts of all I had lost ran through my mind incessantly, like a video on replay. I wept over my loss for weeks but ultimately gained sufficient strength to begin the necessary task of dividing our lives. Closet by closet, drawer by drawer I pulled out items and caressed the memories associated with them. I smelled the aroma of the towels, the sheets, and the room of the one who would never come home again. I grieved as one who had suffered a big loss, unexpectedly and tragically.

My mind took wild rides on the pendulum of thought, wondering if Beth was right and if this was my chance to find a way out of the homosexual lifestyle, too— perhaps God's plan for my escape from the lifestyle that had caused me so much pain. I was again torn between what I knew to be right and what I was told was wrong. I had been taught, and thoroughly believed, that it was healthy to be a member of a church, and I knew that the Bible teaches us to submit to the authority of our pastors and elders out of respect for their calling and their God-given placement. It was out of respect for church authority that I had been compliant so far with plans for our personal transformations.

The first two decrees of the elders, that one of us should move out and that we should have no contact, had come at the lowest point in my life, when I lacked the wherewithal to operate from anything but embarrassment and fear. But I rebelled against the elders' next decree—that one of them should be in attendance when Beth and I separated our belongings. This seemed like an overt invasion of my privacy. When the elders brought it up, all I said in response was, "No, you don't have to do that." I thought their decree came from ignorance and lacked human decency because our relationship had been about love, and these should therefore be very private moments of pain. Although I was incensed, Beth did not object to their request, and so once again I was seen as the one who would not comply.

Finally, the elders relented and allowed us to be alone during this activity. But they made it clear that the visit was to be kept short and focused on the task at hand. The date was set for her to come the following Saturday. All week, my mind drifted to our time together. The chance to see her again, no matter what the circumstances, was enough for me. With each passing hour, my anticipation grew.

As Saturday arrived and Beth walked to the front door, my heart involuntarily skipped a beat. I tried to calm myself as I greeted her. After all, my heart knew what this meeting was for and that my love had left me. But the Beth who entered was not my love. This Beth was guarded and fearful, speaking only of the necessities of the prescribed visit. We were like two actors in a tragedy, one willing to do anything to keep what she had and the other resolved to break free. She quickly agreed with how I had divided our things, and in less than an hour the life we shared was no longer ours but hers and mine. We hugged, and I asked if she would please stay, but she said no. I could not grovel. If this was what she wanted, I would not stand in her or God's way. With our last good-bye, I lost her forever to the ranks of the Christian socially correct.

In the following weeks, only one family from church came to my aid. A husband and his wife, who had been a helper with the Kid's Club, had the wisdom to see that I was not in the kind of emotional state to be left home alone. When I finally told them what had happened, they said nothing about my sin and gave me no looks of judgment. Instead, they invited me for dinner and to stay overnight as often as I liked. On the evenings when I seemed at my worst, they insisted that I stay with them. Even though I had never spoken of harming myself, I knew what they were thinking. They realized it was for God to convict and their part only to love. Despite my grief, one thing was clear: they loved as Jesus loved.

Many nights I went there after work just to avoid going home to an empty house. They welcomed me each time as if I were part of the family, shielding me on my journey, making sure I did not walk too close to the cliff of despondency. Our conversation would revolve around anything but the issue at hand, but more than once I heard them objecting angrily to how the elders were handling my situation and expressing their outrage at the church "leaving me alone in such a state," as they put it.

The elders called their treatment of Beth and me making us go "cold turkey." Through this metaphor they likened us to heroin addicts forced to endure withdrawal rather than people who had been in love. They had forgotten about the beloved Kid's Club workers and the woman with the voice of an angel who sang at worship services. In their places were dirty, addicted homosexuals.

The elders' decree that Beth and I have no contact meant that we could not both attend the church. Since Beth was thought to have found the higher road, I knew she would be welcomed at church while I would forever be looked upon with a wary eye. So I chose to leave; actually, the disgrace had embarrassed me so much that I felt relieved to not have to face the Sunday crowd. I am not sure which decision involved more pain—Beth's to stay and face the questions or mine to leave and face the loss.

I soon decided to go to our sister church that had been established when the church we had attended for almost seven years had grown from two hundred to six hundred members. I had a few friends from the Secret Sisterhood who already attended, so I knew I would not be alone. For the leadership of both churches, this would be a way to know of my where-abouts, with whom I was spending time, and whether I was violating their cold turkey decree.

A loose thread was deciding what was to happen with the Kid's Club. How could the church explain that the two leaders had simultaneously left the Kid's Club leadership without warning? It turned out the church leadership was very interested in damage control.

Within a few weeks, I was called before the elder board. As I arrived at the church, I thought about how this was a place I had been proud to call home, a dynamic group of fellow believers who were helping others find Jesus. But now its facade looked altered; the white brick stood tall and stark, peering down at me with lifeless window eyes. The stairs I had once bounded up with anticipation were now chilled concrete leading me to disgrace. I had been asked to meet the elder board in the upper room reserved for official meetings of the church staff, a place where the leaders usually met for prayer but were now about to administer discipline. I had never been in this room before and, upon entering, immediately realized that I never wanted to be in it again.

I entered alone, a young woman in disgrace. The first sight of what awaited me was more fearsome than I could have imagined. Before me were twenty men, seated, with the gravity of the situation etched on their faces. Some did not even raise their eyes to look at me as I entered. After I was asked to sit, the pastor started the proceeding by asking if I was will-ing to abide by the wishes of the board. I was surprised by this question since I had already done most of what they had commanded without objection. The discussion then focused on church membership. Someone had noticed that I had not become a church member, and this was of their utmost concern. They felt that since they had allowed me to lead a large ministry someone should have been more diligent in checking my membership. They wondered how they could control me if I had not officially joined the church. The truth behind my lack of church membership had nothing to do with my not wanting to submit to authority but with my opposition to their doctrine. I did not believe in infant baptism or in the Presbyterian covenant of believers.

For at least fifteen minutes, the dialogue among the men regarding the dangers they could encounter due to my lack of membership continued while I sat there in silence and disbelief at what I was hearing. My love was gone, my ministry was gone, the church, which was the center of my life, was gone, but no one acknowledged my pain.

They then instructed me to go see the church counselor. I was willing, thinking maybe she would be able to convince me that homosexuality was wrong. It was clear that my community had rejected me; I thought maybe there could be a fresh start. Maybe I could change my social pariah standing. As I rose to go, a few of the men spoke words of encouragement, but not one of them offered to stand by my side in the turmoil. Alone, I walked down the concrete steps to the world outside.

Not even my mother came to my aid. On the contrary, she told me she had often prayed we would break up because I had been a bad influence on Beth. She claimed to have seen Beth struggling and predicted that Beth would be the one the Holy Spirit would convict first. She was sorry for my sadness but sure I would be much happier if I met a nice guy and settled down. She caused me even more grief, making it clear that she could not love what I was turning out to be—homosexual. I was every Christian mother's worst nightmare, and yet I still needed the love of my mother. I tried to hug her, but she recoiled and said, "Get away from me, you lezzy." My heart sank, my lips quivered, my eyes glazed over with tears. I turned away, not wanting to give her the satisfaction of this final crushing defeat. She had drawn a line between us, had taken her stand with the judgmental Christian soldiers. She was clearly disappointed in me, but she was still my mother. That day I made a decision to love: no matter how cruel she could be at times, I promised myself that I would treat her with the love that only God could empower me to give. It was clear that I would never be what she wanted me to be, but she couldn't stop me from loving her the way God wanted me to—unconditionally.

There were two other people who came to my aid in my time of deepest despair: my sister and a co-worker. Instinctively I knew that my co-worker Sue could handle the truth about what I was going through. Once I had revealed the cause of my sorrow, she wrapped her life around me in a selfless display of affection. Sue was a wild and beautiful California soul who knew what I needed most was quiet and support. As the winter turned into summer, I spent almost every weekend at Sue's. She and her husband did for me what no Christians had done—they let me mourn. I spent hours crying and sleeping by their pool. There was very little talking, there was no agenda; there was just time to heal.

By now I had lost forty pounds. Food did not interest me. I might have looked good on the outside, but anyone gazing into my eyes had to know that my soul was desperate. Sue seemed to always know when to talk, when to be silent, and even when to offer me something to eat. She gave freely of her resources and time. The months I spent with her were about taking; in my state, I could give nothing and she accepted me just as I was, hoping only that I would reassure her I saw hope. God knew what I needed. He brought me rest and aid from California Sue. To God, I give thanks. To Sue, I will be forever grateful. To her I owe my sanity.

At the time Sue was supporting me, I began seeing the counselor the church had recommended. I was told that this counselor had helped others escape from homosexuality. I told myself that a woman might have compassion and a new therapy strategy. She at least knew a few gay people, which, as far as I was concerned, put her way ahead of my first counselor.

At our first session, my new counselor greeted me wearing a Bohemian crinkled skirt and well-worn Birkenstock sandals. Her face was average, and her brown hair severely parted in the middle with a straight cut that fell around her shoulders in strands. Her jewelry of large polished rocks lay heavily on her chest and hung down from each ear. At first glance, her image as a Bohemian hippy gave me hope. But I soon realized that her soft and inviting appearance was in conflict with her stern personality.

The beginning of our time together was sprinkled with positive expectations, then as the months rolled on, the same ideas started repeatedly coming to the surface:

🙟 You are attracted to your sex because you feel more comfortable with such individuals.

🙟 Spend more time with men.

🙟 Open up your mind to see them for who they are.

🙟 Maturity will help with this process.

🙟 You may be emotionally immature and not ready for a relationship with the opposite sex.

🙟 Becoming a heterosexual will take a lot of hard work and determination.

🙟 Homosexuality is one of the hardest things to cure.

Although the counselor's advice was essentially the same as I had received before, this time I was initially determined to try much harder. I was prepared to run in the other direction when temptation called.

After many months of spending sixty dollars a session twice a week and repeatedly hearing the same ideas, it was time to say good-bye. I was not cured, but I was willing to be open to the idea of dating men, to try to find one I could love.

In October, my sister invited me to a Halloween party. Having most of the parts of the costume already, I dressed as a clown with white face and traditional floppy shoes. Although I knew very few people attending the party, I was happy to be going out and getting some normalcy back in my life. I mingled and tried to amuse people with small talk, but at a certain point the thought of being there alone, without Beth, crept into my conscience. When I could not hold myself together any longer, I thanked my sister and said my good-byes.

Arriving home around 11:00 pm, I went into the bathroom to get ready for bed. There, before me, was a smiling white face with an oversized red mouth. Something inside me crumbled. The words of a Smokey Robinson song blared mockingly in my mind: "The tears of a clown. When there's no one around." I fell to the carpet, my makeup streaking white across the brown nap, and sobbed hysterically, letting the emotions of eight months of tragedy pour out in the empty house as I had thoughts of suicide. I prayed for relief and for my loving God to comfort me. He heard, and it took only a few minutes for my distress to subside. First my suicidal thoughts vanished; then my tears stopped. I felt alone but peaceful knowing I had hit bottom and that there was no farther down to go.

CHAPTER 18

Emerging from Darkness through Forgiveness

THE SISTER CHURCH WAS A STRANGE MIXTURE of the new and the old. Some members had attended the mother church; some had played on the softball team; and many knew that Beth and I were inseparable friends. I saw their questioning glances, seemingly wondering where Beth was, but I offered no explanation. I now spent Sundays in a place whose most redeeming value was the women of the Secret Sisterhood. They were the ones who sought me out, welcomed me, and supported me.

For months, I could not get through a church service without breaking down in tears of sorrow. Tissues were passed; arms were placed around my shoulders; looks of concern were offered, all tendering hope. But nothing could quiet my inconsolable grief. A few knew the source of my pain, but most did not and did not ask. Perhaps some were respecting my privacy, or maybe they didn't want to know the truth, their sense of self-preservation keeping them from exploring my plight. Regardless, I took their gestures of kindness as all they were able to give. In my loneliness, I was glad to have people I could call friends, but the unspoken lay heavily between us, amplifying my isolation.

As the months passed and my sorrow began to lessen, I spent more time with my friends from the new church, including some guys who were in their late twenties and early thirties. I did my best to put into practice what I had been told in counseling, getting to know the young men and, hopefully, beginning on a journey toward heterosexuality. But none of these men made me want to consider them as potential boyfriends.

As my new life unfolded, it began to fall into a routine, especially on weekdays. The house I once ran home to was now a structure of hollow silence. To counteract dread in my new world, I kept busy. I stayed longer at work; I made plan upon plan of something to do or somewhere to be; I ate dinner with friends. My goal was to arrive home exhausted. With only a few hours left at the end of each day, I found it tolerable to be alone, offering me enough time to think but not enough for my mind to go to a dark place of anguish. I went on like this for months, living life at a fast pace, while some people questioned the wisdom of my rat race and wondered when I was going to stop running. I knew they were right, but living life at a high velocity was my only defense against fully realizing all I had lost. They called it crazy; I called it survival.

As the first year passed without Beth, my friendships grew stronger. Sometimes we would go out as a large group, and other times those of us who had grown closer would hang out in groups of three or four. My camaraderie grew most with Tina and Patti, two women who shared a house only a few miles away. In an attempt to find true friends, I had told them the real reason behind Beth's exodus. Fear of rejection had gripped me, but secretly I hoped these two were also lesbians who would be able to grasp my situation. When I had told them my story, they did not give me looks of surprise or gasp with horror. Instead, the air was filled with contemplative silence. When they finally responded, their carefully placed words left me in a strange state of guilt and encouragement. Echoing all that I had already heard, they agreed that God would have wanted Beth and me to part. But then they quickly went on to say they knew God would carry me through and that they would be there for me until God gave me a clear direction.

The confession of my relationship with Beth did not bring the moment of bonding I had hoped. Instead, I felt shame and disappointment at their declaration of my guilt, and again alone in my journey. But the looks of concern and words of encouragement they had spoken made me realize I should also be grateful that these two were real friends who would be there for me until something better came along.

Tina was a new friend, but I had met Patti ten years earlier. Patti had belonged to a women's Bible study that Beth and I had attended in the home of a mutual friend. There were at least twenty women who attended, but the minute Patti walked through the door Beth and I gave each other a knowing gaydar glance. To any lesbian, Patti was a show-stopper. To me she was the cutest, softest, irresistibly strongest woman I had ever met. In addition to her outer beauty, her quiet, contemplative manner made it evident that her thoughts came from careful reasoning; her demeanor indicated that she was comfortable in her own skin; and her strength gave her an air of unspoken authority. Week after week I watched her as she sat in the same chair next to the couch. At a different point in my life, I would have wanted to know her story, but at that juncture I had found contentment with Beth and had no real interest in pursuing Patti. And so the long-legged beauty remained a mystery outside the boundaries of my world.

Now, several years later, Patti had walked back into my life. The woman whom I considered out of my league was now making it clear that she wanted to become my friend. She was still attractive to me, but I had no place for such thoughts, instead focusing on how thankful I was to have her in my group of friends. No weekend would go by without the gang, Patti included, going to a movie, or out to eat, or to a church event. But at some point a new pattern emerged. No matter when Patti or I arrived, we would often be the last to leave, sometimes remaining hours after the end of the evening's activity deep in conversation. In addition, of all the people who knew the truth about Beth and me Patti seemed to be the most interested in how I felt. Our early discussions centered on my feelings about Beth's sudden exodus. Although Patti continued to take a hard line on the sin of homosexuality, she wanted to know what conclusions I had drawn from my heinous ordeal.

Over the months since Beth's departure, I had arrived at conclusions—about men who lived by the letter of the law and not by the grace of God, men who let the letter of the law supersede love for someone they should have seen as lost, men who should have seen me as Jesus would have seen me, men who knew the teachings of Jesus but ignored the scriptures they had sworn to live by. Jesus had spoken of shepherds searching all night for one lost sheep while the others were safe in the shelter (Matthew 18:10–14). These men should have shown compassion but instead had left me as a sheep, alone, wandering, and vulnerable to the perils of the wilderness.

Although I had always been honest in my opinions, I now refused to hold back, even with those who might have damning powers. Despite my many attempts to live as a heterosexual, the counseling designed to help me, and the many years of prayer for change, I was realizing and embracing my reality. I did not see even the slightest conversion in my soul toward being a heterosexual. I let Patti know these thoughts and many more. I even floated the radical and forbidden idea that homosexuals were born as homosexuals, that God did not make mistakes, that this was not a condition to be "fixed," and that I was not even sure it was wrong.

My conversations with Patti went on for several weeks. Although she could have run to the elders with my heretical thoughts, she retained them in her mind while holding the line on what she had been taught. She rebutted my opinions. She feared my radical views, but she continued to call me a friend. I had been through tragedy, and even though I was afraid to trust her, our weekly talks began to show that she was allowing herself to feel my pain.

Over the course of our conversations, I gained a new maturity and found the strength to emerge from the darkness. Life had shown me the worst emotional pain; if I could get through this trial, I decided I could live through any sentence the church or the world could impose on me. God was still at the center of my world, but I was able to separate him from the confused hatred of humankind. I was realizing that I seemed to be blessed with a new sort of wisdom.

I could tell I was on the brink of a fresh understanding. With each step, fuzzy images of a new way of thought would come into focus and then retreat again. Only one thing was clear: I was seeing a place where I could finally find peace with who I was. Marrying a man was not going to be my answer; being single was not my calling. Over and over the same thought came to me: there had to be another way.

In my new world, I allowed myself brief moments to think that I was to both love God and be myself. In such moments, I would experience my soul bursting open in a flash of freeing light, being in good standing before God and weeping tears of joy. But within moments the teachings of my youth would reach up from the deep, grab hold of my ankles, and pull me down again into the darkness. The battle raged on. How could I toy with the thought of a God who loved me just as I was? How could I question what I had been taught? Could God possibly accept me as one of his servants and also as a homosexual? The answers came back: how preposterous; how prideful; two thousand years of teaching and you, a nobody, are going to proclaim it erroneous? My conscience before God was clear. I was beginning to think I might be right. The white flag of surrender was no longer waving, I was gaining strength for the fight. I knew it would be me against my Christian world. The real battle was just beginning, and in the midst of the clash I was finding peace.

But before I could fully embrace this new world where peace reigned, I needed to take care of my heart. The Bible says that the root of bitterness will spring up if we are unforgiving (Hebrews 12:15). For more than a year, God had told me that I needed to forgive people who had hurt me.

For more than a year, my mind would give grace and then quickly rescind it. It was important that I address my feelings toward those who had hurt me. Although my church and its elders had made some mistakes, I did not blame God. I reminded myself that church members and elders were good men following their beliefs, trying to do what they thought was best. They were still my brothers in the faith; I didn't need to agree with their tactics, but I did need to forgive them.

As for Colleen, the task would be more challenging. I wondered how she could have reported my circumstances to the church after all I had done for her and how I could forgive someone who had taken so much from me. I had only seen her once after Beth left. She had moved into the senior pastor's home. I did not ask why but assumed it was for her protection so she would not fall prey to her own homosexuality. When I asked why she had betrayed my confidence, her face first registered pain then looked sheepish. The only explanation she could give me was that she was asked and had told the truth. For a long time I could not forgive her, although I did not wish her harm. Already she was drowning in a tumultuous sea of oscillating motives and feelings, thinking she had done what God would have wanted and heartbroken that I would never be what she had dreamed.

To forgive Colleen, I needed to remember that I myself had often been forgiven and was not sinless. Since Jesus had died so all sins could be forgiven, who was I to withhold forgiveness? Daily, God brought to my mind the truths of the Bible and the necessity of forgiveness. One year and then two years passed as I slowly released my grip of fury and was able to forgive Colleen. If Jesus could forgive me for all I had done, I concluded, I would forgive as I had been forgiven.

CHAPTER 19

The Final Piece That Brought Peace

AFTER YEARS OF SIMPLY BELIEVING the church's interpretation of the scriptures on the topic of homosexuality, I knew I would have no peace until I discovered on my own what the scriptures truly said. This research, I hoped, would be the final piece of the puzzle that would either bring me peace or hold me in the bonds of celibacy for the rest of my life. The operating principle of the church—"God said it, I believe it, that settles it"—did not leave much room for reexamination of Bible verses. With this principle drummed into my mind for thirty years, I lived a life sure that something had to be wrong with my behavior. My conscience had told me that I was loved by God, but my church had told me that the very basis of my being was wired incorrectly. Now I hoped I could get further enlightenment by revisiting the scriptures. If what I had been taught was true, I could not in good conscience deny the word of God. But if what I had been taught was not true, I could finally allow myself to accept my homosexuality without guilt or shame.

Knowing that the vast majority of Evangelicals believe all reasons for homosexuality are wrong and an offence to God, and realizing that a lot was at stake in my personal life, I opened my Bible to search for the truth. With such an indictment of homosexuality by so many members of the Christian church, one might think that the Bible is full of passages concerning homosexuality, but this is not so. Out of the 66 books, 1,189

140 THE PEACE SEEKER

chapters, and 31,103 verses, only six verses deal with the topic. In taking a fresh look, I knew I had to be objective. If so much as one verse spoke of a loving same-sex partnership in a negative light, I would have to accept that as God's word.

Further, from my theological education I knew I had to interpret all six verses dealing with the topic of homosexuality using three guidelines. The first guideline was to interpret the verse in context—that is, in light of the passages surrounding it. The second guideline was to read each verse with the content of the entire Bible in mind, considering the biblical principles that might apply to the subject. Finally, the third guideline was to interpret each verse in light of the historical circumstances that existed when it was written, assessing whether I was seeing it through the lens of history or imposing the perspective of our modern culture on its content.

When I opened the Bible to determine my future, I was frightened at the potential upheaval the truth of the scriptures might bring. But what I found were facts ultimately supporting my feelings that my homosexual lifestyle was not equivalent to sin in God's eyes, that my conscience had not been wrong. The more I studied the Bible, the more convinced I became that the church's interpretation was not based on careful applications of the guidelines I had vowed to use, and there was even evidence that it was based on nothing more than prejudice. I concluded that without knowing it the twenty-first-century Christian church, which believes homosexuality is a sin, has been fighting the wrong battle. Although such Christians would generally find other types of prejudice despicable, their interpretations of the passages on homosexuality are colored by the prejudice they disdain. Such misinterpretations have, it seems, been passed down through the generations as Christians relied on their pastors or priests to interpret the scriptures and guide their behavior and morality. Then over time, these layers of misinterpretations solidified into an impenetrable granite slab.

Some will believe the truth of what I have found, having perhaps al-

THE FINAL PIECE THAT BROUGHT PEACE 141

ready suspected it as true, while others may find it impossible to believe that their church leaders have been fallible. Personally, I have had to come to grips with the fact that my church leaders who thought they were correct had had good intentions but were not correct in their interpretations. The truth had set me free.

Of the six verses that speak of homosexuality, three are in the Old Testament (written before Christ was born) and three are in the New Testament (written after Christ died). The first passage tells of the twin cities Sodom and Gomorrah. It is a story of unabashed cruelty, grotesque debauchery, horrifying depravity, and human wickedness (Genesis 19:5). The central verse and surrounding verses that add context relate how a godly man named Abraham had a nephew named Lot, who also believed in God and knew God's laws. Lot and Abraham traveled together as nomads, but when their flock of sheep grew too large for the land to support them, they split up. Lot noticed that the land around the cities of Sodom and Gomorrah was fertile, so he told Abraham he wanted that land for his portion. Lot knew that the people of the cities were wicked, but the draw of the culture lured him. As time went on, Lot became more involved with the people of the cities, spending time away from his flocks and eventually taking up residence within the city limits of Sodom. Although aware of the risks of being influenced by its decadent culture, he ignored them, calling Sodom his home. Despite living there, Lot remembered the laws of God, so when one day two strangers passed him at the city gate he recalled the tradition of offering travelers lodging, food, and safety. Lot perceived that these were angels, and he wanted to protect them from the criminals among whom he lived. He took them home and fed them, but before they could turn in for the night the wicked men of the city surrounded the house and demanded that he throw his visitors out so they could rape them. Lot offered his virgin daughters, but the men of the city insisted on Lot's male visitors. The angels helped by striking the men blind and leading Lot, his wife, and his daughters out of the city before God destroyed both Sodom and Gomorrah.

I had always been taught that this was a story proclaiming the evil and sinfulness of homosexuality. But now I wondered how it was possible to equate the action in the story with men being lovingly attracted to other men or women being lovingly attracted to other women. Instead, I realized that this was a story about evil, domination, and hatred, a tale about sin without conscience. Regarding the context of the story, it is clear that the whole city is evil, and this story is not among other passages pertaining to homosexuality. In totality, it is a story of the salvation of Lot and his family, a godly family extracted from the evil that surrounded them.

The scriptures clearly express why God was so upset about Sodom and Gomorrah, although somehow Evangelicals have ignored the truth. I found four other passages that revealed to me what really angered God sufficiently to destroy the cities (Deuteronomy 29:22–26; Ezekiel 16:49–50; Isaiah 1:10–17; Jude 7).

When I discovered what the scriptures had to say about the real sin of Sodom and Gomorrah, I gained confidence, realizing this famous passage was not about homosexuality as we know it. From the first defining verse in Deuteronomy to the last in the Book of Jude, the facts about Sodom and Gommorah were laid bare and differed radically from what we had been taught. The Bible spoke for itself: "The people of the twin cities did not seek justice. They did not defend the fatherless and the widow. They did not encourage the oppressed. They did not believe the truth about God. They paraded their sins. They worshiped other gods. They were happy about wickedness. All were evil. They were full of pride. They were overfed and unconcerned with the needs of others. They were not willing to repent. God was not on their minds. They never stopped doing evil. They seduced the unstable. They were sexually immoral and perverted. Now this was the sin of Sodom: she and her daughters were arrogant, overfed and unconcerned; they did not help the poor and needy. They were haughty and did detestable things before me. Therefore I did away with them, as you have seen" (Ezekiel 16:49–50).

Historical information about facts revealed in these verses also supports a different interpretation from that of Evangelicals. In ancient times, male-to-male rape was used as a means of domination. A conquering army would further humiliate its enemies by the practice. Male-to-male rape was and still is clearly defined as mastery by sexual assault.

Having gained courage from what I found out about Sodom and Gomorrah, I then read, in the book of Leviticus in the Old Testament, the second and third verses that pertained to homosexuality (Leviticus 18:22 and Leviticus 20:13). I focused on these at the same time, because they are interpreted the same way by Evangelicals and others of the Christian church. The book of Leviticus was written by Moses to the nation of Israel. It is called Leviticus because it was named after Levi, the father of one of the tribes of Israel. God appointed this tribe as the priests for the nation. The book is a written account of the offerings to be given to God, the laws of cleanliness, and the laws regarding conduct of the people of Israel and their priests. I again adhered to the guidelines of context, content of the entire Bible, and history.

The second and third verses relating to homosexuality read as follows: "Do not lie with a man as one lies with a woman; that is detestable" and "If a man lies with a man as one lies with a woman, both of them have done what is detestable. They must be put to death; their blood will be on their own heads" (Leviticus 18:22, 20:13). These verses are frequently used as weapons against homosexuals. But again, it was clear to me that they can only be interpreted this way when they are not understood in the light of context, the entire Bible, or historical circumstances.

To focus on context, I read chapter 18 of Leviticus, which consists of a series of verses about who people should not have sex with: "Your father's wife; your father's sister; your sister; your daughter-in-law." Leviticus 18:22 clearly states that if you are a man you are not to have sex with another man; it is detestable. But what I had never noticed before was that the previous verse alters its meaning: "Do not give any of your children to be sacrificed to Molech, for you must not profane the name of your God, I am the Lord" (Leviticus 18:21). Up until this point, the chapter lists those with whom people are not to have sex with. Then Leviticus 18:19 through Leviticus 18:21 focuses on the abomination of the nations living around the Israelites. It seems clear that Leviticus 18:21 and Leviticus 18:22 are a pair—they tell us not only what people should not be doing but why they should not be doing it. The practice of male-on-male sex was associated with the worship of the god Molech. The word *detestable* is not used to set male-on-male sex apart as worse than all other "thou shalt nots." I knew that in the scriptures the word *detestable* was associated with idol worship. The context is a list of dos and don'ts for the nation of Israel.

Throughout the Bible, all forms of idolatry are hated by God. Historically, it is the time for the Israelites to enter the Promised Land. God gives them laws to follow to keep them apart from the other nations that already inhabit the land. Idol worship, with its sexual sacrifice, was forbidden. I had to conclude that Leviticus 18:22 was not a condemnation of homosexuality but a condemnation of idol worship.

Now it was time to take a fresh look at the verses on homosexuality in the New Testament. I had sat through many sermons condemning and shaming homosexuality using Romans 1:26–27: "For this reason God gave them over to degrading passions: for their women exchanged the natural use for that which is against nature. And in the same way also the men abandoned the natural use of the woman and burned in their desire toward one another, men with men committing indecent acts and receiving in their own persons the due penalty for their error."

The background for the verse is that the book of Romans was written by the Apostle Paul to the early Christian church in Rome. Christianity was one of hundreds of religions practiced by the Romans. The belief that

Christ was God and the Savior of the world was new. Paul wrote to these new believers to help them understand that all people in the world were guilty of sin but that their faith in what Jesus had done on the cross would release them from their bondage. He also says that creation is a visible testament to the glory of God and that man should acknowledge God for what God had created. But I wondered where the verse about damnation of women having sex with women and men having sex with men fit into Paul's thought process. All became clear when I read the preceding verse, Romans 1:25: "They exchanged the truth of God for a lie, and worshiped and served the creature more than the Creator." The practice of having same-sex partners had always been part of idol worship, and God had always found it "detestable," but the Roman Empire raised this practice to a new level. In Rome all sorts of sordid behavior was not only accepted but condoned and promoted. "They were filled with all unrighteousness" (Romans 1:20). Thus the type of behavior described in the book of Romans is the lowering of moral standards to the level of sex with any and all. According to the context, I realized that Romans 1:26–27 did not describe homosexual sex between committed partners but instead sex in the basest of forms—random, anonymous sex between any and all.

The next two passages I also grouped together as they are almost identical: "Know ye not that the unrighteous shall not inherit the kingdom of God? Be not deceived; neither fornicators, nor idolaters, nor adulterers, nor effeminate, nor abusers of themselves with mankind" (Corithians 6:9) and "Now we know that the law is good, if one uses it lawfully, understanding this, that the law is not laid down for the just but for the lawless and disobedient, for the ungodly and sinners, for the unholy and profane, for those who strike their fathers and mothers, for murderers, the sexually immoral, men who practice homosexuality, enslavers, liars, perjurers, and whatever else is contrary to sound doctrine . . ." (I Timothy 1:9–10 ESV). In considering the context of the verse, Paul speaks of lawsuits between Christians. Following this verse, he says that thieves, covetous, drunkards, revilers, and extortionists will also not inherit the kingdom of God. In a triumphant statement, Paul goes on to say that "such were some of you." He speaks of all these sins as if they are things people "do," not who people "are"—sins that could be dealt with and banished from their lives.

Regarding historical circumstances, Corinth was the Las Vegas of its time—what was done in Corinth stayed in Corinth. But even though Corinth was a wild city, to understand the culture you would have to know about the religions of the day. Religious practices then were not trying to hold back the tide of immorality; the religion of the day *was* the immorality. The spiritual life of a Corinthian centered on the temple, and the foulest of sexual perversions took place behind the temple doors.

Looking into the original Greek, I discovered that the word *effeminate* here in Greek is *malakia*, meaning literally "soft." Jesus used the same word to describe fine cloth. In ancient Greece, the word referred to males who had the "feminine" characteristic of being obsessed with their appearance. Their perversion was seeking to be sexually dominated by all who were willing participants. The sin of these men, who were considered weak-minded, would have been wanton sex, being ruled by their sexual agenda rather than God. The practice of being sexually dominated came from temple worship and became part of the everyday lives of the Corinthians. Although this verse does speak of same-sex partnering, once again dominance and idol worship are the context.

Investigating one more word, the Greek *arsenokoites*, a combination of the words for "man" and "bed," would either set me free or make me bow to the teachings of my youth. In English, this phrase seemed to be saying that men who slept with other men were abusing humankind, but the Greek word sheds a different light on the verse. *Arsenokoites* means to force sex on a weaker party. Regarding historical circumstances, we know that the practice of pederasty—an adult male taking an adolescent as his lover for pleasure as well as social status—was prevalent when the New Testament was being written. The advances of an adult male were to be considered flattering; but to the young man who did not have a choice in the relationship, the sex could be better described as rape. Although the sexual domination of the older over the younger was accepted in the culture, Paul spoke strongly against this practice for Christians, advising that pederasty was not love but a sin against the body, and that practitioners of it were "abusers of themselves with mankind."

There is no way to deny that I Corinthians 6:9 is speaking of male-on-male sex, but there is also no way to deny that it is also speaking of sexual practices that are extreme, nonconsenting, or out of bounds for God's people. To focus only the homosexual acts in this verse is to miss the point. What it was really saying is that this is a list of what God considers "out of bounds," including the sexual abuses of both homosexuals and heterosexuals. The *malakia* and *arsenokoites* are grouped with "the adulterer" and "the fornicator." Ultimately, I realized that this verse is not speaking of love among two people of the same sex, homosexuals who love and are committed. Rather, it is speaking of sex as domination; sex with someone other than your marriage partner; sex with any and all who are willing or nonwilling participants—sex as lewd behavior.

Consequently, what had for me started as fearful research of Bible passages ended with a bold belief that God had created me and loved me just as I am. I could now live without guilt imposed by others. I had fully considered the context of historical facts related to the Bible verses pertaining to homosexuality. I would not allow the errors and prejudices of others' interpretations bind me in shame and sin.

These six verses and surrounding passages that had been used as weapons against me and countless other homosexuals were now keys to accepting myself for who I was, no longer a second-class citizen of the kingdom of God. As a lover of Jesus, I could at last hold my head high and say that I was just as much one of his servants as every other believer who sat next to me on Sunday mornings; I belonged. I had discovered the last piece of the puzzle, the most important piece, and it had finally brought me peace.

It was time for me to share what I had discovered. I needed to plead with Christians to look again at the Bible verses traditionally used as weapons against homosexuals. I had lived a life in secret outside the doors of real fellowship while well-meaning church leaders held these six verses as their weapons of truth. I knew it would be difficult to change minds, but I had to try to convince the world of the truth I had found. I had discovered the cause God had called me to champion.

CHAPTER 20

Experiencing the Sunshine of Acceptance

FOLLOWING MY SELF-ACCEPTANCE after coming to terms with Bible verses related to homosexuality, my slowly evolving relationship with Patti led to my unexpected acceptance by members of my church community, giving me a new sense of belonging. Our developing relationship was initially complicated. For ten years or more, Patti had been pursued by a young man, Tim, who had started to attend our church. They had first met early in their careers, and their love of horticulture and laughter had resulted in a lasting friendship. A large, good-looking football-player type, Tim was employed as a landscaper. We all knew Tim believed that he and Patti were meant to be together; he was just patiently waiting for her to come around to the truth. Tim's persistence made Patti wonder if she was being foolish not to give the relationship a chance. Finally, they dated for a few months, but it didn't take long for her to realize that even though she loved Tim as a friend the relationship was not going to bloom into love.

With his plans now dashed, Tim turned to Tina as an appealing candidate. When I first met Tina, she had been full of life and laughter, a creative dreamer bordering on eccentric. Strong and athletic with an entrepreneurial streak, she seemed to have big ideas about ways to generate money and success.

At the time, Tina and Patti were still living together, and I could only imagine the upset brewing in their household behind closed doors. Tina did not want to hurt Patti's feelings, but she also could not pass up an opportunity to find love. What ensued was the most uncommon of courtships. Tim and Tina rarely spent time together. Some people chalked this behavior up to their being a bit older and carrying their independence into their romantic life. However, I surmised the real reason for Tina's behavior—that she knew she was gay and felt conflicted—but I kept it to myself. The months went by, and the couple that seemed no more than good friends became engaged and began making wedding plans. Still questioning the true nature of their relationship, I told myself that I was reading my past attempts to have romances with men into their lives. Patti was upset at the news but would not say why. I wondered if it was because she was losing Tina or because she was losing her to the perfect catch she could not bring herself to love.

As the wedding date approached, Patti and I, already spending a lot of time together, were to become best friends. The ever-quiet, measured, and deep-thinking Patti finally revealed to me that Tina had a past with women and that she grieved for Tina, having cautioned her about the huge mistake she thought she was about to make. Patti, without telling an unsuspecting Tim the truth about Tina's past, also tried to warn him about a marriage she was sure would end in disaster. Instead of understanding Patti's warning as it had been intended, both Tina and Tim interpreted it as an expression of envy at their approaching marital bliss.

More warning signs about problems with Tim and Tina's relationship appeared as time went on. For example, on one date they went to a local park for a bike ride. Tim wasn't much of a biker; as an ex-football player, his weight had made him unexcited about getting on a small object with rubber wheels. But Tina had wanted him to share her love of biking. Anybody who knew about this date was a little skeptical. But the ride didn't end like we thought it might. It was Tim who called the emergency room. Tina had experienced a persistent stabbing sensation in her lower abdomen so intense it had made her vomit. The diagnosis was a ruptured fallopian cyst. After a few days, Tina had recuperated and their dating resumed. Several months later, as their engagement was announced and the wedding grew closer, the rupturing began again. Reflecting on my own ordeal with stomach pain years before, I wondered if Tina's body was trying to warn her, rebelling against her plans to marry Tim.

Yet their wedding plans continued. The night of the bachelorette party, I joined the Christian revelers to send the bride-to-be off to her wedding and honeymoon. Tina was clearly nervous, but one of her best friends tried to cheer her by joking about the blindfold and vodka she had packed for Tina to make it through the wedding night. I was horrified. While her family and friends cheered Tina on, I remained silent and worried.

Finally, the wedding morning came, with the entire world seemingly happy at the joining of Tim and Tina. The sky was a brilliant blue; the sun shone clear and warm; the air felt light. The guests filed in with smiles and quiet laughter, all sharing anticipation of the bridal procession. The music started, and we rose in unison to honor the bride. There Tina stood at the back of the church, a beautiful bride arm in arm with her father. But something was not right: Tina was in tears. She wept all the way down the aisle and throughout the ceremony. I am sure others attributed it to overwhelming joy, but from my perspective it seemed more like watching a lamb being led to the slaughter, but I told myself I was overreacting. I was so uncomfortable that I wanted to stand up and shout, "Stop—don't do it," but it was not my place to speak up. The wedding that had started with family and friends rejoicing ended with a bride standing at the altar with her soul laid bare, her face shrouded in tears.

Ultimately, over the years of their marriage the couple suffered because of Tina's sexual orientation and decision to marry. The first month of marriage, they started arguing and never stopped until a respite occurred in their third year when they had a beautiful son. But soon after the joy of his birth, their bickering would resume. One year followed another, and the Tina who had once been so full of adventure slowly deteriorated, her laughter subsided, her zest for life vanished. By the eighth year of marriage, the couple's arguments turned to bitterness and finally complacency; they now had a marriage of coexistence. By the fifteenth year, Tina knew she had to do something or she would forever lose herself in depression and despair.

One day, Tina, a ghost of her former self, sat in our backyard, her body slumped, her eyes brimming with tears. Fear and determination gripped her as the words spilled from her lips in what she thought would be a new revelation: "I'm gay. I tried to do what God wanted, but I just can't take it for the team any longer." With this pronouncement made, she sat there ashamed but relieved that the pain of all of the years would soon come to an end. Although her confession was not unexpected, I felt nothing but compassion for this friend who had taken such a damaging path.

Tina had believed with all her heart that she needed to squelch her homosexual desires, that the Bible said acting on her gay feelings was a sin. In her effort to please God, Tina had done what she thought was right. Now she was confused about her conflicting beliefs, but she did know she could not go on living a lie. She had loved Tim, but it had not been the kind of love that should have led to marriage. Tina, who had loved God and followed him since her teens, ended her marriage because she could no longer live a life of falsehood. I saw Tina and Tim's story as another example of lives shattered by the church's teaching on homosexuality.

At various times, seeing Tina's confusion about her sexual orientation highlighted some of the experiences Patti and I were having. Patti continued to speak to me about her belief that homosexuality was evil and a sin. But although she verbally rejected the homosexual lifestyle, her actions seemed to suggest otherwise. The strengthening bond between us made even the roughest days sweet with the thought that she would be there for me. We were now rarely apart, and no task seemed too small for her to offer help. Although she had made her opinion clear, I knew if the circumstances were different I would want more. I continued, however, to make sure my actions were in accordance with her words. I simply would not let myself go toward someone who said being gay was wrong. Having found peace in my belief that God loved me just the way I was, I would not settle for any partner who could drag me back to the torture of indecision and shame, who was not convinced and at peace with who they were before God. Additionally, the loss of Beth was still a fresh wound, and I did not believe that I could live through another profound emotional injury.

In August, my sister invited me and a guest to her annual summer picnic and to stay the night. It was far enough from home that a late-night drive after a full day of festivities was not desirable. I invited Patti, shoving thoughts of sleeping with her as far from my conscious mind as possible, telling myself this was not what Patti wanted and that it would not happen.

When we arrived, the deck was packed with my sister's friends, drinking beer and conversing. The sun was high as I made my way around the crowd greeting people, then sometime later I realized I had left Patti alone in a group of strangers. Scanning the crowd, I was relieved to see her on the far side of the deck talking to my sister. They were both looking toward me, but there was an expression on Patti's face that I had not seen before. Gone was the guarded look that seemed to express no interest in me. Patti's mask had momentarily slipped, and her eyes told me what I had suspected for months—that she was in love with me.

When we turned in for the night, we did sleep together, but we did not have sex. Instead, we confessed the frightening truth that we were in love. The next morning, I woke up scared about pursuing a relationship with Patti. If Patti really believed all she had said to me about the evils of homosexuality, how could I trust her with my heart? During our drive home, she told me she knew her feelings toward me were wrong. But this time her words lacked their usual believability. I was not sure where this relationship was headed, or whether I was willing to take a chance on love again. The situation was weaving a tangled web of emotions within me.

Over the next year and a half, Patti maintained her belief that a relationship with me would be wrong. We played our parts: me wanting to pursue a commitment, her heading toward one then backing away. My heart was guarded; I would not fully give it away till she made up her mind to be all in or gone forever. On several occasions, we vowed to stay apart only to realize neither of us could bear to think of life without each other.

By the second year of our tumultuous bond, I had had enough. I loved Patti and knew she loved me, but I could not go on with life in our constant state of upheaval. As another summer faded, we spent a weekend at the Jersey Shore. In the evening we walked the boardwalk with the thousands of other tourists, ducking in and out of the many shops that sold everything from ice cream to beach sundries to fine jewelry. In the jewelry store, I found a sapphire and diamond ring I liked and half-heartedly asked Patti to buy it for me. I was looking for a commitment and told myself it was now or never, though what I really believed was that our relationship would end soon. If Patti could not reconcile her gayness with God, I would not continue to hold her back from what she believed to be true. We left the jewelry store with no ring. The rest of the evening Patti was quiet, deep in thought. I told myself we were soon to part and that, although it would hurt terribly, at least I would be able to move forward in my new reality.

In the morning, Patti told me she had not slept because all she could think about was the ring. I was surprised at her reaction, but maybe I should have known how heavily my request would lay on her mind since she never took decisions lightly. She had to consider and reconsider all aspects and possible aftereffects when making any large purchase, so one that came with a commitment would take even more consideration.

That afternoon we took a walk on the beach. Even though we were surrounded by thousands of vacationers lying in beach chairs and frolicking in the water, we were alone. The same silence from the night before hung between us. With each step we took, sadness deepened its hold on me; with each stride I became more resigned to a lifetime apart. We walked on the harder sand along the water's edge; we walked through the puddles collecting from foamy waves; we walked around the remnants of sand castles left to be demolished by the sea. Patti was still silent, as was I, sure that I had ruined the weekend with my request. Then suddenly Patti sat in the powdery tan sand at the ocean's edge and broke her silence. In a nervous but sure tone, she said she had decided to buy the ring. I tried to object by saying I didn't want to pressure her, but she insisted that she was going to buy the ring and that it would represent her lifetime commitment to me, a marriage together through thick and thin. She went on to say that although she was not completely convinced about God's acceptance of homosexuality, her belief about its being a sin had been changing. She asked me if I would be willing to be patient with her as she continued to work through her belief about homosexuality in relationship to God and the church. Her speech, though short, had the weight and sureness of an oath.

My fear and sorrow turned instantly to joy. Patti had made a proposal, and I happily accepted. We were two nervous yet confident people who had made a decision to love. Just a few hours later, we purchased the ring with all the ebullience that any couple starting life together should experience. My life was beginning again; I had found a new forever love.

When Tim and Tina left for their honeymoon, Patti moved into my townhouse with me. It was perfect timing for averting suspicion: Tina had gone on to wedded bliss, and Patti needed somewhere to live. But once again a veil of secrecy had been placed over my life. Tina, though she had chosen to move on, was beside herself with the thought of Patti and me together. When Tina tried to counsel me on the phone, it fell on deaf ears as I had heard enough speeches about the sin of homosexuality. What I could hear loud and clear was her jealousy. It seemed her words were spoken not out of concern but rather in an attempt to try to drive a wedge between Patti and me. However, I had decided I would let no one rob me of my peace again.

Although I had found peace with the God I loved, Patti was on her own journey. I did not try to convince her of the truth I had found, believing she would need to find self-acceptance and peace with God for herself. If I was wrong about believing that God loved me as I was and didn't wish me to change, I certainly did not want to bear the responsibility for having led her down a path of error.

As it had been for me, Patti's changing relationship toward her sexuality was a long, slow spiritual journey. At first, she knew only that she loved me. She wasn't sure how God felt or what our relationship would mean for her spiritual life. She had not become a follower of Christ until her teens; nevertheless, she had witnessed firsthand the devastation that could result when our church caught someone living a homosexual lifestyle. Fear made her insist that the church should not know, our friends should not know, and her family also must be kept from ever knowing the truth.

For Patti's sake, I had reverted to closet living at my place of employment as well. Once again the "we" in conversations became "I." I did my best to refrain from speaking of my home life for fear that someone would ask about my husband or children, and from engaging in conversations that otherwise would have been a natural gateway to my co-workers' lives. Once again I felt walls being erected and the distance that secrets put between us and others we care for. I had now been promoted to manager of fifteen women and was afraid of them finding out—or worse, protesting or making up some story about me being inappropriate. I watched my every action carefully to avoid doing anything that might even remotely cause alarm. Since the topic had not come up with senior management, I also feared the unknown. I was sure they would not fire me for being gay, but I didn't know if they would make my life more difficult, and I didn't want to find out.

As five and then ten years passed, our love grew. Even though Patti remained closeted, I started to become more vocal about my sexuality. Although I would never have flaunted the truth, I decided to no longer lie. If someone asked or if an occasion required me to bend the truth, I was not willing to further the ruse.

No longer wanting to live a lie and yet still terrified of others knowing the real me, I lived each day with a seesaw mentality. I had hopes that a time would come when I could overcome my fear and tell a co-worker I thought I could trust. But when such a moment finally came it wasn't anything like I had imagined. It was not a hushed moment when I daintily traipsed out of the closet of my own accord. Instead, it was more like having the closet door ripped off its hinges and hurricane-force winds pummeling me from behind.

The management team at my place of employment was away at a retreat in the Pocono Mountains. In the evening, we were treated to a fine dinner in the stately lodge's main restaurant. The large round tables each sat twelve, and, as luck would have it, both my boss and the company-hired retreat facilitator were seated at my table. I do not know if he was trying to impress my boss or if he just took joy in trying to break down barriers between people, but soon after we sat down the facilitator proposed a means of breaking the ice, asking people at our table to describe their partners and their most special attribute. Right there in the midst of the white linen and fine silver, panic gripped my heart. I had to decide whether or not to confess to my peers the homosexual lifestyle I had kept so tightly guarded. One by one, my fellow managers told their stories. One by one my turn grew closer. My heart pounded in my chest, but I told myself I would not lie; fear of their response had to be secondary. Soon the men and women who worked by my side all sat waiting, looking at me. Gone was my usual bawdy slapstick as I said, apologetically, "I hope this does not bother anybody, but my special someone is a woman named Patti." I started to go on, but my boss, feeling the weight of what I was divulging, interrupted. Seeming to shield me with her power, she said with conviction and authority, "It will not be a bother or a problem to anyone here or anyone in our company." Her kindness was a sudden burst of sunshine through rainclouds—the sunshine of acceptance. Relief replaced worry, and I was able to enjoy the rest of the meal peacefully as if my manager's words had been a grace said before eating. After dinner at the bar, I tried to blend in, but compliments on my bravery and the encouragement of my newfound friends kept me the center of attention. The closet door had been blown off, and so far I liked it.

Yet the more that people came to know the truth about me, the more Patti remained closeted. I urged her to relinquish her fears, but her dread of rejection was strong. Weekly we discussed this and would tussle verbally, with two themes repeatedly emerging. First, neither of us was willing to lose a church home. We had seen gay friends, as a means of compromise, drift into churches that didn't speak of the Bible, believing that if they were not accepted in fundamentalist churches they would find a place where they could still worship. We acknowledged that we would rather remain closeted than be left starving for spiritual nourishment.

Second, we both wanted to be Christian witnesses, to live our lives as mirror images of Jesus, allowing others to see the kindness and love of Jesus in us. I tried to convince myself that in time people would see we were truly Christians who were also gay, but Patti repeatedly pointed out that the vast majority of the world would not understand that someone could be gay and a Christian. I, too, had that fear but did my best to hide it, hoping that one day everyone would know that homosexuality and Christianity were not diametrically opposed. Years passed with us still far apart on the two subjects that kept Patti closeted. But we both knew it was only a matter of time until she would be thrust out in the open by sheer association with the woman whom she had pledged to love forever.

When it was time to buy a new house together, we started to discuss going to a new church where no one knew us. But this time we decided that Patti would go to one church and I would go to another so we could still worship each Sunday without watching eyes ever guessing the truth about our home life. I reluctantly went along with this plan and was soon worshiping regularly at a local church near our new home while Patti had also found a church she loved. Week after week, I tried to fit in at the church I was attending, without much success, while week after week Patti would tell me of the wonderful people she had met at her church. Eventually, curious to see it for myself, I asked if I could go along just once, and halfheartedly she agreed. After one visit to Patti's church, I was hooked, impressed by the powerful worship, terrific teaching, and vibrant atmosphere, and I knew immediately that her church was where I wanted to be.

Patti's dream of attending church with no fear had vanished, but matters got worse when our vision of going to church where no one knew us also vanished the first week I arrived. Patti had been attending this church for over a year, but she did not know that the associate pastor, whose name was John, was a fellow graduate of mine from the second Bible college I had attended. The minute he stepped on the stage to lead the singing, I recognized him. Although he had been nothing more than a classmate, I had always admired him from a distance for his gentle way and quick smile. Now as I watched him play his guitar, it was obvious that his shell of conformity had cracked, and a man wearing a T-shirt and baggy jeans, sporting a scruffy goatee had emerged. Gone was the organized, fundamentalist Bible-thumping approach to Christianity that had been drummed into us at school. The person standing before me now was not only a man who loved God but a better man who was doing his best to separate what he had been taught from what he was finding to be the reality of a Christian life.

Even though John posed no immediate threat, the thought that he might know someone who knew of my past made me nervous. I watched as Patti waged a tug-of-war with herself, pitting her fear of excommunication against her excitement at my decision to stay. We both did our best to ignore our fears, happy in our new surroundings and proud to be part of a cutting-edge community of believers. Wanting to be involved, Patti began helping in the nursery during Sunday School, while I approached the pastors for permission to begin a Helping Hands ministry, linking church members with skills to others with needs in the community.

Apart from sitting with each other every week at worship service, we did our best to appear as friends who simply attended the same church. Five years passed, and, although our fears never allowed us to be truly ourselves, we were happy that we had found a place capable of helping us become more like Jesus. Week in and week out, all was well until I was once again contacted by the pastors, this time not by phone but by email, the new technology of terror. The email, which was from John, read: "I would like to meet you for lunch as soon as possible. We are wondering how you and Patti had been received at church." Each word seemed an invitation to a death sentence. All the familiar feelings surfaced—fear, dread, upset—but this time I was prepared, as if I had known the day of reckoning would eventually come. I told myself that if they asked I would tell the truth. I had been kicked out of church before; I would live through it and move on. As for Patti, this was the first time she had been involved in a call from pastors. We both shed tears at the thought of being cast out of the place we had both grown to love.

John and I arranged to meet two days later at a restaurant near the church. The low ceilings appeared to close in on me as we were ushered to a table in the dining room and seated. The dark wood of the booths seemed to seal me in like a coffin as I awaited the death of yet another portion of my life. John was his usual chatty self, spending an hour or more talking about everything under the sun from music to books he had recently read. It was torturous waiting for the true reason for our meeting to begin. Since I needed to get back to work, I signaled for the check, whereupon John finally shifted to the topic I feared. He began by asking how others in the congregation had treated Patti and me. I looked at him quizzically, mumbling something about all being fine. He confirmed, "We assume you are together?" The moment of truth had come. Without flinching, I said, "Yes, we have been for thirteen years." I steeled myself for his next statement, but rather than speaking John sat silently, his shoulders relaxed, his eyes pooled with tears; then he reached across the table, placed his hands on top of mine, and said words that I never thought I would hear in my lifetime: "We want you to know it is okay with us. The leadership team has discussed it in depth, and I have been sent here to tell you that Patti and you are welcome at our church. We want you there."

Another hour passed as John revealed how his own gay older brother had left the church, feeling ostracized, and how the church leadership had spent months of discussion and prayer coming to a decision about us. Apparently, the leadership team had battled for several years with people from the congregation who had asked judgmentally, "What are you going to do about them?" All the while, Patti and I had been oblivious to the war that had been raging within the congregation. Eight or ten people had already left in protest. I felt terrible hearing that they had left and about the turmoil the pastors had endured on our behalf. Patti and I did not want to be a reason for divisiveness in the church, so I suggested we leave to stop the upheaval, but John would not hear of it; he said he would not want to be a pastor to those who would not allow some-one to come to church.

As our meeting drew to an end, John asked if Patti and I would be willing to meet with him and the head teaching pastor later in the week. Without hesitation, I agreed, knowing that I owed these men a great debt. They had done the unimaginable: by standing up for those whom most thought were sinners. In disbelief, I wondered if a dream had come true, if a lifetime of shadows was truly being bathed in the bright sunshine of acceptance.

Walking on a cloud of euphoria at the thought that someday the closet could be a thing of the past for homosexuals, somewhere between the restaurant and my car I realized I was experiencing a relief that was not just emotional or mental but also physical. My whole body seemed lighter. When I called Patti from the car and recounted the conversation, she could not believe what she was hearing—that we were welcome and wanted, that the truth had set us free.

Subsequently, we invited John and the head teaching pastor, Allen, to our house for dinner. The evening was spent reiterating the long journey they had taken to gain acceptance for us among the leadership team. They had both spent the past months rereading the scriptures regarding homosexuality and questioning the interpretations they had been taught to believe.

John was further along in his acceptance, while Allen, although believing no one should be barred from the church, was still struggling with the idea of homosexuality being a sin. As we told him of our separate journeys, his realization that we were indeed Christians who shared all the doctrines regarding Jesus as our Savior gave him more to ponder.

In the following months, the appreciation for what these church leaders had done for me sank deeper into my soul. I had been living as a second-class citizen of our church community. With the backing of the pastors, I now experienced being a full-fledged member of the church community, and I began making great strides in my spiritual life. Acceptance had given me permission to walk more closely with God. I felt gratitude for a God who loved me just the way I was and for the men who had risked their own comfort for two women whom they knew needed to have a church home. The words of an old hymn perfectly described what had happened to me: "My chains fell off, my heart was free. I rose, went forth, and followed thee."

CHAPTER 21

Pioneering Reconciliation

A FEW MORE YEARS PASSED, and other than an occasional conversation with Pastor Allen about homosexuality and the church, all was quiet. No one else had left the church except John, our champion, who, after years in the pastorate, had left to seek employment as a carpenter. We missed him, but the church went on, with several new folks joining and all feeling a sense of community.

Peace and harmony reigned until it was announced that our next teaching series would be in the Book of Romans. I felt the old familiar dread, knowing the verses in the first chapter of Romans were the ones that most churches used as a platform to call homosexuality a sin. When the Sunday came for Allen to teach from the first chapter of Romans, I could see from my third row seat that this usually calm, eloquent speaker was anxious. I whispered a quick prayer as Allen took a deep breath and bravely told the congregation of the common interpretation then went on to say that in his research he could find no support for it, instead believing that when the Bible spoke of homosexuality it was mostly in the context of dominance and the practice of same-sex partners in idol worship. He went on to say that he did not think the Bible spoke of the loving relationships of same-sex partners, adding, though, that he personally believed marriage was only between a man and a woman. But by the time he had gotten to his conservative view of marriage no one seemed to pay attention anymore to what he was saying. All they had heard was their pastor being soft on homosexuality. Allen had dropped a bomb, and within hours his phone was ringing, resulting in demands that he spend weeks in conference with church members.

Once again, Patti and I were thrown into the conflict. This time we had not started the upheaval, but in the eyes of some church members we were guilty by association. Wanting to be strong in his convictions, Allen had spoken what he believed, yet now he could not help but be fearful for his congregation. Fifteen or twenty key people left the church, unable to abide what they thought was a turn toward liberal teaching on homosexuality. After confirming that this exodus was due to his teaching and to us, and unable to bear the thought of being part of the reason for divisiveness in the church, Patti and I resolved to leave it ourselves.

To discuss the situation, we requested to be present at a leadership team meeting. As we arrived in the dimly lit room, there, already seated on plush couches, were the people who had risked themselves for what they thought were the true teachings of the scriptures, their weariness attesting to the trials they had experienced in the past month. Patti and I sat in silence, knowing that what we wanted most was to relieve their pain.

Allen spoke first, recounting how many had barraged him with questions and had left the church. We had not realized the depth of his tribulations until he finally wept in frustration. To him, they were beloved friends who would no longer be worshiping with us. Then in a sorrowful voice Patti told the team that we would be leaving the church. In an instant, one of the ladies said, "No, you can't leave." And immediately all agreed that if we left, everything would be for naught. A line had been drawn. One by one, they elaborated on their reasoning, indicating how the leadership team was divided on the topic. Some did not believe the lifestyle Patti and I led was wrong, while others called it a sin. But even though they were divided, all believed that no one in the congregation had a right to bar us or any other homosexual couple from worship.

If homosexuals weren't allowed to come to church, who would be targeted next? Even though they had not found total agreement with our lifestyle, their words reflected both the wisdom of Solomon and the love of Christ. Finally, we acknowledged that the leadership team was right—we could not leave. We had been instrumental in pioneering a new way of thought and agenda, advocating reconciliation between the congregation and gay church members. No matter how hard it was for us, it had been much harder for the leadership team who had taken up our cause. For their sake and for the sake of all gay people who sat secretly in worship around the globe, we agreed to stay.

But the meeting was not over. Allen had one more topic to address. In his discussions with the people who had questioned his teaching on homosexuality, one issue had repeatedly been raised: most who thought homosexuality was a sin believed we should be allowed to come to church but that I should not be permitted to lead the weekly adult Bible study. Since the Bible teaches that leaders are to be "above reproach," Allen had to ask me to step down from this position. I agreed, but I had one condition: I was doing it for them, not because I believed I should not teach. God had given me a gift of teaching, which I would lay aside until I could teach without causing divisiveness.

The weeks passed, but I could not bring myself to tell the twelve people who regularly attended Bible study that I would be stepping down. My heart was heavy as I knew I would soon not be able to experience the elation I felt in preparation and delivery of the word of God. It was as if a blanket had been thrown over the fire in my soul. Even though I was doing it for the good of the church community, I could not help but acknowledge to myself that I had once again become a second-class citizen. Nevertheless, this church had given me much; now it was my turn to give.

We still attend the little church we love, flaunting nothing, hiding nothing. Some church members fully accept us; others remain on the path to understanding. In the Christian church at large, the battle rages on, while the world itself has asked those outside the church to offer gays equal rights. I believe the Christian church will rise once more to fight for what it believes to be true. The casualties may mount as the church continues along its path of ignorance, never realizing that the ones they denigrate sit secretly among them. I can only hope that its eyes may one day open to see what it has really taught for centuries: God loves us just the way we are. As for me, I have been wounded in battle, but I still worship and serve the God I love, who has given me peace.

CONCLUSION
Becoming a Peace Seeker

Gay, *lesbian*, *bisexual*, and *transgender* are now commonplace words in the English language. Nightly news, movies, and talk shows all seem to have at least one segment or story line regarding gays. The gay marriage issue has burst onto the national scene with a passion equal to that of the civil rights movement. Amidst this focus on the issue, the majority of Americans have gone from opposing gay marriage to acceptance, a transformation that has occurred faster than for any other social issue of our time. It has amazed me to watch the states wrestle with laws and, one by one, ratify or revise them in favor of gay rights. I would not have believed this could happen ten years ago. A new movement has begun to topple bigotry, to set one more class of people free.

From the standpoint of the average American, all seems to be going well for gays. The American public would largely say they are proud of where our nation is headed concerning equal rights for gays. They would say their hearts have been softened as they have seen the joy of same-sex couples who have waited so long to be accepted. What they are seeing and feeling is the equality, freedom, and happiness that are the very basis of our American way of life.

But while the media streams stories about cultural freedom for gays into our homes, another force continues its opposition to equality and acceptance for gay people. This force is strong and sure, and its army sits in pews, millions deep. This is the conservative Christian church, unmoving in its conviction that homosexuality is a sin. The American culture may have changed, but by and large the stance of religious institutions has not. The Christian church feels a responsibility to stand for its belief that the Bible is infallible and its interpretation of the Bible is true. When Christians say that homosexuality is a sin, they think they are stating a biblical truth, and they want to speak the truth as they believe it, to counter the tide of the new America.

In opposition, the media does its best to portray the Christian stance on homosexuality as old-fashioned and bigoted. And many Americans are angry at established religion, fueled by disappointment and distrust of the hypocrisy they see in priests and pastors who have sexually abused children or traded God for money. All of this leads to the conclusion that the Christian perspective on homosexuality is prejudice wrapped in a package of old-fashioned doctrine. The teachings of the Christian church need to be changed. A day must come when no one will feel forced to sacrifice what they know to be true about their sexual identity because of what they have been taught is a sin.

The church has not yet begun to rally against the legalization of same-sex marriage. After all, we have not seen the church's leadership storming the halls of Congress in opposition to it. Pehaps its silence is fueled by a belief that our nation has surrendered to depravity. But whether or not the church applies pressure on Capitol Hill or tries to sway the Supreme Court, it remains strong in its condemnation of homosexuality. As a result, it will continue to train its army, and the war will go on.

If church members continue to be taught that homosexuality is a sin, there are only two possible scenarios for future generations of Christians. In one scenario, individuals of the next generation will not see homosexuality through a lens of prejudice. They will view two people who love each other not as evil but as two loving individuals. Already the next generation does not emphasize the differences previous generations could not seem to ignore. This next generation will love God and be able to differentiate between people who sin and people who were made the way they are by God. They will revive the true Christian church doctrines once more, making them strong again by getting rid of bigotry and errant teachings that have stood for so long. This is my hope and wish for future generations.

But sadly, the second possible scenario seems more likely. In this scenario, the Christian church will continue to espouse interpretations of the Bible rooted in prejudice against the homosexual lifestyle and will remain a place where homosexuals are not accepted. It is possible that the next generation of people who are brought up in the Christian church will simply renounce their faith due to teachings they cannot condone because they see the church as therefore irrelevant and purposeless. The next generation, gay or straight, will not go to a place they do not believe teaches what they know to be right. Instead of holding on to what is good and doing their best to ignore and fight on, gay Christians will dismiss the church and, along with it, the God who loves them.

The future of the church is in our hands. Christians need to seek God and ask him what he would want from his followers. We must set aside history and tradition and look once more at the Bible and its inherent truths. We must realize that lives are at stake, that many have chosen suicide rather than face the battle at hand.

People who do not believe in the God of the Bible also have a part to play. They must comprehend what causes the conflict between homosexuals and Christians, then give grace and understanding to those trying to follow what they have been taught. Knowledge will bring awareness, and awareness will bring insight.

My greatest hope is that one day Christian homosexuals will be able to love God free from secrecy, free from second-class citizenship, and that one day gays will be loved as they are and not ostracized for something they did not choose.

The war wages on. Together we must all seek peace.

RESOURCES

Readers seeking more information about the conflict between homosexuals and Christians, or wanting to help resolve it, may find the following resources helpful.

Books

Bible, Gender and Sexuality by James Brownson (William B. Eerdmans Publishing, 2013)

The Cross in the Closet by Timothy Kurek (BlueHead Publishing, 2012)

God and Gay Christian by Matthew Vines (Random House, 2014)

Is the Homosexual My Neighbor? by Letha Dawson Scanzoni and Virginia Ramey Mollenkott (HarperCollins, 1994)

Stranger at the Gate by Mel White (Penguin, 1995)

Torn: Rescuing the Gospel from the Gay vs. Christian Debate by Justin Lee (Jericho Books, 2012)

Organizations

Believe OutLoud
Believeoutloud.com

Evangelical Ecumenical Women's Caucus (EEWC)
PO Box 78171
Indianapolis, IN 46278
Eewc.com

The Evangelical Network
PO Box 324
Pacifica, CA 94044
Theevangelicalnetwork.net
info@theevangelicalnetwork.net

The Gay Christian Network
Justin Lee, Executive Director
PO Box 17504
Raleigh, NC 27619
919-786-0000
Gaychristian.net

Just Because He Breathes: Learning to Truly Love Our Gay Son
Rob and Linda Robertson
Justbecausehebreathes.com

To learn more about the author
or to inquire about her availability as a speaker,
please visit her Web site at:

WWW.THEPEACESEEKER.COM